Buying a Property ...

Thank you for buying one of our books. We hope you'll enjoy the book, and that it will help you to realise the ideal combination of a place in the sun and a rising investment.

We always try to ensure our books are up to date, but contact details seem to change so quickly that it can be very hard to keep up with them. If you do have any problems contacting any of the organisations listed at the back of the book please get in touch, and either we or the author will do what we can to help. And if you do find correct contact details that differ from those in the book, please let us know so that we can put it right when we reprint.

Please do also give us your feedback so we can go on making books that you want to read. If there's anything you particularly liked about this book – or you have suggestions about how it could be improved in the future – email us on *info@howtobooks.co.uk*

The Publishers
www.howtobooks.co.uk

If you want to know how...

Buying a Property in Spain
An insider guide to realising your dream

Going to Live in Spain
A practical guide to enjoying a new lifestyle in the sun

Buy to Let in France
How to invest in French property for pleasure and profit

Living & Working in Portugal
All you need to know to enjoy life in Portugal

Retire Abroad
Your complete guide to a new life in the sun

howtobooks

Please send for a free copy of the latest catalogue:

How To Books
3 Newtec Place, Magdalen Road
Oxford OX4 1RE, United Kingdom
email: info@howtobooks.co.uk
http://www.howtobooks.co.uk

The Daily Telegraph

Buying a Property in Portugal

*An insider guide to buying
a dream home in the sun*

SUE TYSON-WARD

howtobooks

To Edie, the first of Mummy's books for you.

First published in 2004 by
How To Books Ltd
3 Newtec Place, Magdalen Road
Oxford OX4 1RE, United Kingdom.
Tel: (01865) 793806. Fax: (01865) 248780.
email: info@howtobooks.co.uk
http://www.howtobooks.co.uk

British Library Cataloguing in Publication Data
A catalogue record for this book is available from the British
Library

Illustrations by Nickie Averill
Cover design by Baseline Arts Ltd, Oxford
Produced for How To Books by Deer Park Productions,
Tavistock
Typeset by PDQ Typesetting, Newcastle-under-Lyme, Staffs.
Printed and bound by Cromwell Press, Trowbridge, Wiltshire

NOTE: The material contained in this book is set out in good
faith for general guidance and no liability can be accepted
for loss or expense incurred as a result of relying in particular
circumstances on statements made in the book. The laws and
regulations are complex and liable to change, and readers should
check the current position with the relevant authorities before
making personal arrangements.

Contents

Acknowledgements

I would like to thank the following people for their help and guidance in the preparation of this book:

David Littlewood, Kate Rimmer and Andrew, Peter and Una Maddison, Robert and Jan Wood, John and Joyce Davison, Clive Willis, Ann and Harold Greenhalgh, Barbara Baird and Graham Tyldesley, Bill Collis, for all their thoughts on the buying process and life in Portugal; the UK Portuguese Chamber of Commerce; AFPOP; Peter Ward, for his valuable information on properties and their defects.

Many grateful thanks, too, to Nikki Read at How To Books, for her patience during the difficult gestation period of this book, and my husband and parents, for keeping baby away from the keyboard long enough for me to do some work!

1

Why Portugal?

FIRST THOUGHTS – CAN SO MANY PEOPLE BE WRONG?
Port wine, sardines, tea-towels, the ubiquitous cockerel
symbol, sandy beaches, golf, football and the spectacularly expensive legs of Luís Figo: all these are typical
Portuguese images and icons – and of course there's more,
much more. Mention Portugal in conversation and many
people instantly conjure up warming memories of sun-
filled days in languid enjoyment of the increasingly
popular holiday destination – the Algarve. In 1999, 27
million people visited Portugal, almost 12 million of these
as holiday tourists, outnumbering native inhabitants of
the country! The vast majority of visitors come from the
UK (now accounting for almost 2 million annually),
Germany and Spain, and a steady influx from the USA
(around 3% of visitors), Canada and Brazil.

They are all drawn to the sun, the relaxed way of life, cheaper prices (although these are changing since the introduction of the euro), beaches, the landscapes of the north, and the good, cheap wine and food.

In addition to this constant transient swelling of numbers each year, thousands have gone on and bought property in Portugal, mostly as holiday, or second homes, but some also as a permanent move, either for retirement, or a new way of life. It is estimated that in 2001 the number of British people who bought property in Portugal rose by 25%. Whilst Spain continues to tempt the greatest number of British ex-patriots, Portugal enjoys growing popularity, especially amongst young families, and the retired, and an estimated 50,000 people now enjoy residence there.

A huge 48% of all tourists to Portugal stay in the Algarve, and indeed many go on to make their homes there, with about 20% of Algarve residents now British. With average sunshine rates of 8.6 hours a day, and a much better all-round climate, it's no wonder the southern coastline is a PR person's dream commodity. For those who have ventured beyond the foreign, ex-patriot enclaves of the Algarve (even by a mere 5 km or so), Portugal has also offered much more than sun, beaches and golf: a varied landscape, a fascinating history, good food, family values, a calm lifestyle, and above all, the warmth of its welcoming people – a true hand of friendship and a feeling of belonging.

If you are considering making your visits to Portugal more permanent, it is worth pondering carefully the primary factors in your decision-making. This book, as well as containing guidance on the process of purchasing property, and life in Portugal, also contains comments and case studies from people who have actually taken the plunge and done it for themselves. Hopefully, you will feel inspired, but also cautioned by their tales, and you will take a more balanced view of what is involved. The extensive reading and contacts lists at the end of the book should give you extra starting points for research.

ENGLAND'S OLDEST ALLIES

The English are made most welcome in Portugal because we have long enjoyed a special relationship with our more southerly counterparts. England and Portugal boast the world's oldest friendship alliance, dating back to 1386, and sealed by such links as the marriage of the Portuguese João 1 to Philippa of Lancaster, daughter of the Duke of Lancaster, John O'Gaunt. One of their sons, Henry, was to become the well-known Prince Henry the 'Navigator', a title bestowed upon him by the English. It was these early English connections which had facilitated the help of English archers against the Spanish in the battle of Aljubarrota. In fact, many traditions which we consider quintessentially English, such as drinking tea, and eating marmalade, came to us via the Portuguese courts, through the marriage of Catherine of Bragança to Charles II. During the Peninsular Wars of the early 1800s against Napoleon, Portugal once more relied upon British intervention to rout the French leader at the famous battle of the Torres Vedras lines.

Things have not always been so cosy. After assisting Portugal to rid the country of Napoleon in the 1820s, British power in Portugal led to much unrest, and eventually gave rise to the Liberal movement there. Even 40 years later the English, who now had a stronghold in the port wine industry in and around Oporto, dictated external affairs in Portugal. However, apart from a few periods of unease, the link between the two countries has been steadfast, with both enjoying mutual respect. In World War I Portugal was reminded of its Alliance, and under British influence, finally joined the Allies, having initially taken a neutral stance. For further background on this intriguing part of European history, you must read the two gripping novels set in Portugal by Robert Wilson: *A Small Death in Lisbon* and *The Company of Strangers (HarperCollins)*. See Reading lists on page 217 for details of these, and other books of interest.

Today, those old ties remain firm. The English are made to feel welcome in Portugal, although it is probably true to say that the British lager louts are as unwelcome here as anywhere. Luckily, Portugal (and the Algarve in particular) still manages to attract a large number of families, so drunken excesses are, on the whole, blissfully less obvious than in some Spanish and Greek holiday hotspots.

ZÉ POVINHO (JOE PUBLIC) AND HIS LIFESTYLE

Personally, I have mostly been treated with kindness and respect, especially when the Portuguese discover I can speak their language, and most people I talk to say the same. Speaking Portuguese really does open up doors to you. Sometimes initial encounters can be difficult; the Portuguese can occasionally be somewhat dour, officious and intransigent. But with a bit of gentle persuasion, when they do open up, you are treated to friendship and extreme kindness. It is not uncommon, for example, when asked for directions, for a Portuguese person to actually escort you to where you want to go to make sure you do not get lost en route. On one occasion in Lisbon, my husband and I had been having a snack in a café-bar and got chatting to the owner. He proceeded to take us round the nearby church to show us its splendours, paid our entry to the adjoining museum, and finally insisted on treating us to port wine and a tour of the lavish Port Wine Institute round the corner!

The Portuguese are justifiably proud of their tolerance, their ability to form lasting friendships, even on different sides of the world, and their place in history as discoverers and shapers of the world as we know it today. Their self-acknowledged 'soft customs' (*brandos costumes*), have won them many friends in return, and despite their sometimes helpless resignation in the face of problems, and lack of speed and logical planning, their honesty and warmth prevail. They are traditional people, but whose modern generation also embraces new developments with facility and keen spirit. They are staunch exponents of family values, and the extended family network is still of vital importance, even though, in other aspects of life, modern developments continue to take place. More women now work, have fewer children, have more rights, and take their place amongst Europe's educated and dynamic new generations. Modern technology has taken a hold in Portugal, having one of the highest rates per head of population for mobile phone-owners, although the number for computers per household is still low compared with other EU countries. In rural areas, the old traditions hold fast, and life in huge swathes of the country has not yet caught up with the pace in the larger cities. There is still poverty. Whilst you might drive along super highways built recently with EU funding, in the same vicinity a farmer may be ploughing his land with oxen, or threshing corn using outdated manual methods. So Portugal maintains its curious mix of idyllic charm and exciting modern advancement, which is probably one of the reasons why it has such wide appeal.

For a delightful account of life in typical rural Algarve, you must read the two books by Ruth Banks, long-term resident there: *Wild Herbs and Happiness – Life in an Algarve Mountain Village (Books 1 and 2)*. The books are available in bookshops in the Algarve.

CLIMATE

Sitting where it does, on the westerly edge of Europe, with a coastline of around 800 km, and extending approximately 500 km down through predominantly Atlantic climes towards a more Mediterranean atmosphere, Portugal has a vastly differing landscape, which has not altered much since the initial establishment of pre-historic features such as the imposing granite deposits in the northern and central highland areas, and the soft rolling plains of the south. Although it has a natural border with Spain in the form of a line of mountains and long rivers (such as the Guadiana), Portugal actually shares many geographical and geological features with its neighbour. The climate changes too, in the same way as it does in Spain. From the wetter northern atmosphere, with concentrated rainfall in the fertile hilly and coastal regions (the most northern coast is called Costa Verde – the Green coast), down through protected central areas, whose summers are relentlessly hot in contrast with freezing winters, and finally to the idyll of the south coast, whose mild climate is so coveted by northern Europeans, although as world climates generally continue to change, even the Algarve has provided unsuspecting visitors with surprise downpours in the middle of hitherto sacrosanct warm periods. The Portuguese island groups of the Azores have a temperate climate, whilst Madeira is subtropical round the year.

AVERAGE TEMPERATURES: C/F

For more information on the different regions, see Chapter 2.

Region	Jan	Feb	Mar	Apr	May	Jun	Jul	Aug	Sep	Oct	Nov	Dec
Lisbon and Coast	14 57	15 59	17 63	19 67	21 71	24 75	26 79	26 79	25 77	22 72	18 65	16 60
Costa de Prata	10 50	11 51	13 56	15 58	16 60	18 64	19 66	19 66	19 66	16 62	14 56	11 52
Costa Verde	9 49	10 50	12 53	13 56	15 59	17 63	19 67	20 68	18 65	15 60	12 53	10 50
Plains	13 56	15 59	17 63	20 68	24 75	29 84	33 92	33 92	29 84	23 74	19 63	13 56
Algarve	15 59	16 60	17 63	20 67	23 74	26 79	29 84	29 84	26 79	23 74	19 66	16 60
Madeira	18 65	19 67	19 67	20 68	21 70	22 72	24 75	25 77	25 77	24 75	22 72	20 68
Azores	14 58	14 57	14 58	15 59	17 62	19 66	21 70	22 71	21 70	19 67	17 62	16 60

source: ICEP

AVERAGE RAINFALL (MM)

Region	Jan	Feb	Mar	Apr	May	Jun	Jul	Aug	Sep	Oct	Nov	Dec
Lisbon	114	79	112	57	47	19	6	7	36	65	92	106
Costa Verde	162	115	152	89	90	44	23	29	54	108	151	171
Mountains	152	107	136	76	72	45	18	19	42	82	113	147
Algarve	73	55	75	34	24	8	4	4	20	54	68	70
Madeira	67	77	82	36	21	8	3	3	28	79	92	87

THE LANGUAGE

Portuguese is a language of Latin origins, with some influences from smaller groups of settlers, such as the Moors. It has been claimed on numerous occasions that it sounds like Russian, and certainly the intonation bears a resemblance, even though the written form is more akin to a mixture of French and Spanish. What the vast majority of people do not realise is that Portuguese is not simply the language spoken in their holiday destination it is also a very important world language. It is a wonderfully rich and diverse idiom spoken across four continents by approximately 200 million native speakers. Portuguese is in fact the third most spoken European language in the world, behind only English and Spanish, and overall in the world league-table lies 6th or 7th (the debate still goes on about the top two or three, but without doubt it is far more widely spoken than French, German or Italian).

To many Portuguese native speakers their language

represents their whole cultural heritage, and its prolific spread around the world is linked to their early world expansion and domination. It is the language of Brazil, the African countries of Angola, Mozambique, Guiné Bissau, Cabo Verde and São Tomé and Príncipe, East Timor, and was once the main language of Macau. See Chapter 11 on how to learn Portuguese before you go, and once you are there.

PROS AND CONS OF LIFE IN PORTUGAL

As mentioned, there are many advantages to life in Portugal. In addition to those already touched upon, comments from those who have made the move include:

- climate/low prices at the time of buying
- loved the place and the people
- winter sunshine/Portuguese very friendly and helpful/ did not want to depend on flying
- good base to holiday by car in other European countries
- still a relatively safe place, especially to raise a family
- lots to do in tourist areas
- buying procedures in the Algarve are made easy by the number of English-speaking agents and lawyers
- cheap flights to the Algarve
- lifestyle allows time to be with the family
- realistic house prices (in north), good weather, friendly and helpful people, less crime
- access to lots of golf!

But before we get over-excited about the possibilities, let us temper the hype with a modicum of reality and common sense. Of course there are cons too, and throughout this book we shall explore the pitfalls as well as all the positive factors. I'll give you a few starters to think about:

- bureaucracy
- utilities – such as lack of piped gas, mains water, long waits for telephone lines
- slow pace of life – can be TOO slow for some
- different type of leisure activities/lack of many customary amenities
- driving…!
- climate – can be very hot in summer and damp or freezing in winter
- integration – not always easy without a knowledge of the language
- isolation in rural areas
- employment situation not easy in every region
- economy currently in recession.

These, and many more will be discussed in later chapters.

SUMMARY

Portugal is *the* choice for millions of holidaymakers, and thousands more constant/permanent visitors, and is certainly an option well worth considering if you are planning to buy property overseas. There are many positive aspects of life in Portugal, and it compares favourably with other European countries in terms of its cost of living and easy lifestyle. It is a welcoming country, and its people are particularly open to families, and anyone who makes an effort with the language and cultural integration. The climate and more relaxed approach to life are major pulling factors for many people. But it pays to look at the whole picture; after all, an investment in property is not a cheap step to take. It is worth thinking carefully before you go any further. We hope by the end of this book, you will have a better idea of whether Portugal is the place for you, and of how to go about safely buying your dream property, and living the life there you want.

2

Planning Where to Go in Portugal

Although the vast majority of people buy and settle in the familiar Algarve, Portugal has a lot to offer in its other regions, away from tourist areas, or in the bustle of large cities such as Lisbon and Oporto. The Algarve is a safe bet for most people, as it may have been their host for holidays, or they may have friends there already. The comfort of an established ex-patriot community may be of benefit to some, especially in the first few months of settling down, but it may never be more than that: ex-patriot – a small piece of Blighty in the sun. For the braver, and those willing to integrate more fully into Portuguese life, venturing away from these apron-strings will be rewarded with fantastic areas of natural beauty, mainly cheaper prices, and a taste of the real thing. In general, house prices in Portugal have been steadily increasing since 2002, particularly in the Alentejo, but spectacularly so in the luxury market in the Algarve, which has also had an effect on prices overall in the south.

Before you make any judgement, you should approach this with an open mind, and endeavour to visit a couple of different regions, at different times of the year, to fully appreciate what there is on offer. You can always fall back on the security of the Algarve, and even there, if you want to get away from it all, you can quite easily find tranquillity a few miles away from the tourist hot-spots. The next chapter looks at types of property and weighs up location pros and cons in more detail, but here we take a tour of the regions, and show you what each has to offer.

AN OVERVIEW OF THE REGIONS

Portugal today has five administrative regions:

- ◆ Norte
- ◆ Centro
- ◆ Lisboa and Vale do Tejo
- ◆ Alentejo
- ◆ The Algarve.

These represent areas of the country with distinct characteristics, from the industrial north, with the highest number of the population, encompassing the wine-growing lands but also the isolated mountainous areas, down through the rugged and coastal central regions running into Lisbon and environs, the second largest region in terms of population. From the Tagus valley the

The five administrative regions of Portugal.

country opens out into the sprawling plains of the Alentejo – the predominantly agricultural region – the largest in land mass, housing only a fraction of the population. The final area is the Algarve, with its tourist and golfing developments on the coast, interspersed with smaller, still typical villages. In addition, Portugal counts as its territory the two autonomous Atlantic island groups of Madeira and the Azores (*Açores*). Mainland Portugal is further divided into 18 administrative districts, with smaller municipal and parish districts within them.

The provinces of Portugal.

However, ask a Portuguese person where they are from, and it is highly likely they will refer to the province from which they originate. Portugal was originally divided into 11 such provinces, the names of which are still used by inhabitants and still appear in many tourist information and guide books. As the provinces themselves vary in geography and culture, so too the people who live there differ in appearance, character and background. The contemporary (Nobel Prize winning) writer, José Saramago, when asked to define the Portuguese in the BBC Discovering Portuguese programme, famously said that a Portuguese person from each province was very different from the next, and that he would probably die before working out what was the true Portuguese character!

COSTA VERDE AND MONTANHAS (NORTE)

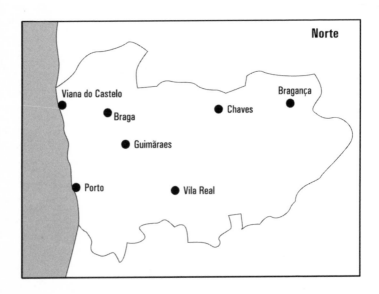

The NORTH comprises the provinces of **Minho**, **Douro** and **Trás-os-Montes**. The Minho borders on to **Galicia** in Northern Spain, and there are many overlaps, in culture and language across the frontier. The Minho is one of the lushest areas in Portugal, with a climate and landscape similar to that of a damp, northern European country. It's no wonder its coastal line is called the **Costa Verde**. The area produces the popular 'green wine' (young wine) *vinho verde*, both red and white. The Minho houses the country's largest National Park, **Peneda Gerês**. The north is steeped in traditions, and is very religious and hard-working. To the east, the Minho is flanked by the mountainous region of **Trás-os-Montes** (literally translated as behind the mountains). This is an area isolated geographically from the rest of the country, rugged in landscape, very poor, and whose towns and lifestyles are still somewhat reminiscent of Medieval Europe. Its people however are fiercely proud of their heritage, more Celtic in nature than much of the country, a legacy of northern invasions. The main industrial area in the north is the **Douro**, whose river runs down from Spain (917 km from source to coast), providing the vital font of life along the long valley from the surrounding hillsides down into **Porto** and the wine lodges (*caves*) on the riverfront at **Vila Nova de Gaia**. There are many links with the British, most of which are still visible today in Porto, the country's second largest city (Oporto is the anglicised name for it, it is in fact O Porto = the port). About 1.3 million people live in and around Porto, participating in the many busy commercial activities of the area which, in addition to viniculture, also include the production of ceramics, cotton goods, sardine-canning and some farming. The coastline stretching from the Douro southwards is popular with holidaying Portuguese, although Atlantic winds keep temperatures to a less tolerable level than in the Algarve at certain times of the year.

FACT FILE

Region: Costa Verde and Montanhas (Norte).

Provinces: Minho, Douro, Trás-os-Montes.

Main towns and cities: Porto, Viana do Castelo, Braga, Guimarães, Bragança, Chaves, Vila Real.

Industry/Economy: wine industry, canning, agriculture, shoes and cotton goods, copperwork, gold and silver, embroidery and lace.

Typical food and drink: tripe, trout stuffed with ham, sausage and black puddings, Port wine, vinho verde, thick soups, feijoada bean stew, Portuguese casserole, sweet cakes, caldo verde kale soup, Monte cheese and bottled mineral water.

Things to do and see: Peneda Gerês national park, Douro river and wine estates, tours of wine cellars in Vila Nova de Gaia, Bom Jesus shrine and steps, wild countryside, Mateus palace at Vila Real, coastal resorts such as Ofir, Póvoa de Varzim, Espinho.

Transport links: São Bento station Porto, links with express trains to Lisbon and south and north to Vigo and Galicia; airport; good IP highway from Vila Real to Bragança.

Types of property: rustic farmhouses, town centre apartments, seaside flats and town houses, with or without businesses, typical rural stone-built houses with steps up the outside and space underneath for animals/vehicles, some traditional windmills.

Prices: apartments in Oporto area from €5,000+/on the coast 3-4 bedroom flats at €135,000+, and detached country houses from €275,000+.

Further info: Tourist Office Porto – Praça D.João 1, 43, 4000 Porto. See also lists in Directory.

COSTA DE PRATA (CENTRO)

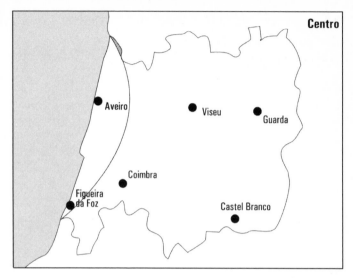

The CENTRAL provinces include the three **Beiras (beira** means edge or river bank) – **Beira Alta** (higher), **Beira Baixa** (lower) and **Beira Litoral** (coastal). Of these, Beira Litoral is home to a number of towns of great historical interest, including the beautiful city of **Coimbra**, Portugal's equivalent of Britain's Oxford and Cambridge. With a population of around 80,000, it is one of the largest cities in Portugal (only Greater Lisbon and Greater Porto count over 1 million residents), and is well-known for its university, founded in the 13th century, and its cape-clad student singers of the doleful *Fado* song. On the coast are various traditional fishing towns, whose fishermen sometimes still use oxen to pull their brightly coloured boats up the beach, and whose inhabitants still indulge in numerous rituals to accompany the blessing of those boats. The interior of the region is built predominantly from granite, with some amazingly rugged landscapes.

There is some small-scale farming here. The **Serra da Estrela** divides Beira Alta from Beira Baixa.

Region: Costa de Prata (Centro).

Provinces: the Beiras (Alta, Baixa and Litoral).

Main towns and cities: Coimbra, Aveiro, Castelo Branco, Guarda, Viseu, Figueira da Foz.

Industry/Economy: water bottling, bedspreads and rug-making, wine, fishing, farming, salt production, paper-making, some tourism, crystal and glassware.

Typical food and drink: Serra cheese, suckling pig, Bairrada and Dão wines.

Things to do and see: Serra da Estrela mountain range, ski resort and hunting lands, Aveiro lagoon, Monsanto (Portugal's most 'typical' village), Buçaco forest and spas, Conímbriga Roman ruins, Coimbra, border castles, shrine at Fátima.

Transport links: small rail network, local bus links, A1 motorway passes near Coimbra and IP5 fast route, many roads are smaller, very quiet with uneven surfaces.

Types of property: distinctively striped beach houses, granite-built country properties, more modern town houses and flats.

Prices: rustic ruins in need of work from €25-30,000/ rural cottages from €45,000. Flats on the coast from €100,000 and larger villas at €300,000+.

Info: Região de Turismo do Centro, Largo da Portagem, 3000-337 Coimbra. Plus Directory.

LISBOA AREA

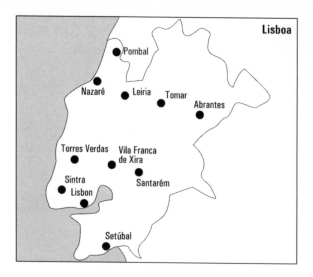

Around LISBON, the provinces of **Estremadura** (Lisbon and the coastal area), so called as it was considered the 'extreme' part of the Roman Empire and **Ribatejo** – 'along the bank (ribeiro) of the river Tejo', sit shoulder to shoulder, supporting the capital and Greater Lisbon catchment area where approximately two million people live (almost one million in Lisbon itself). Lisbon has shot to popularity as a location for business investment, and now is home to many well-known foreign businesses, including hi-tech companies, on a growing number of business parks. It is also highly rated as a spot for city breaks, especially amongst the affluent young in search of a lively nightlife. Lisbon is fashionable and in more than one way is the real hub of the country. The Estremadura area encompasses the lands surrounding Lisbon, taking in the breathtaking environs that are the setting for the picturesque towns of **Óbidos** (rated the most perfect

Portuguese town, because of its preserved cottages and town walls) and **Sintra** (adored by Lord Byron), as well as the popular resorts of **Cascais** and **Estoril**, once-fashionable summer destinations of European aristocracy. Beyond these, to the west, juts out the **Cabo da Roca**, Europe's most westerly point, and the crashing Atlantic waters host world windsurfing contests. To the east of Lisbon, the province of Ribatejo stretches up along the **Tagus valley**, a highly fertile land where the fighting bulls are bred for Portuguese bull-fights.

FACT FILE

Region: Lisboa area (Lisboa & Vale do Tejo).

Provinces: Estremadura and Ribatejo.

Main towns and cities: Lisbon, Setúbal, Sintra, Leiria, Nazaré, Santarém, Tomar, Vila Franca de Xira, Torres Novas, Torres Vedras, Abrantes, Pombal.

Industry/Economy: hi-tec/ IT, tourism, salt, fishing, ports, agriculture and bulls, ceramics, wine, leather.

Typical food and drink: fish and seafood, wine (including sweet dessert wines), Sintra cheesecakes, custard tarts from Belém, egg-sweets.

Things to do and see: Lisbon has many attractions, including St George castle and Oceanarium on former Expo site, palaces in Queluz, Mafra and Sintra, the coast and natural reserves at Sado and Tejo locations, churches at Alcobaça and Batalha, horse fair in Golegã.

Transport links: Airport, trains, excellent coach network, good motorways with link across Tagus by bridge, boats and ferries.

Types of property: city centre apartments (old and new), modern flats on outskirts, new luxury complexes, white-washed houses in country areas, large former summer residences.

Prices: extremely variable. Flats from €150,000 and larger from

€200,000. Studio-type flats outside the centre from €75,000. Large houses with pools (mostly on new developments outside Lisbon) €400,000 to in excess of €1 million. Cheaper south of the Tagus: new 2-bedroom flats from €100,000, rising to €190-500,000+ for town houses and modern builds.

Info: Tourist Information: Palácio Foz, Praça dos Restauradores, 1200 Lisboa. Plus Directory.

THE PLAINS – PLANÍCIES (ALENTEJO)

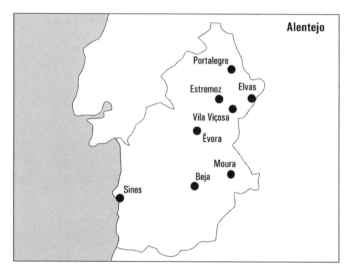

Ribatejo gives way to the immense provinces of the ALTO and BAIXO ALENTEJO. These rolling plains of **oliveiras** (olive trees) and **cortiça** (cork), and vast expanses of open land are sparsely populated – a staggeringly low 20 people per square km, compared with approximately 278 in the Lisbon region, and 166 in the north. The Alentejo ('away from the Tejo') has always suffered as a region, despite its dominance in size. The land itself is not particularly fertile, and has been a struggle to farm, although the area is known as the *Celeiro de Portugal* (the granary of Portugal), due to its cereal production. It is also here that cork is grown to supply most of the world's demands. Prior to the 1974 revolution the area was divided into large estates, called *latifúndios* (*latifundia*) owned mostly by absentee landlords and worked with outdated methods by the locals. After the revolution in 1974 the estates were taken over and run by workers' cooperatives, but EU subsidies are still needed to help out the large rural communities existing there. Marble (*mármore*) is a valuable commodity quarried in and around the capital of the region, the historical town of **Évora**, and particularly at **Vila Viçosa**. Some of the small neighbouring towns produce some of the best red wines you will ever taste, and the town of **Arraiolos** has found world-wide fame for its hand-made tapestries and rugs (*tapetes*). The whole area, especially the **Baixo Alentejo**, has had a historic link with Communism – in fact it was from here the 1974 revolution was instigated – and tends to be less religious than in the north. The lower hills roll over into the rural Algarve, and houses become more typically Moorish, white, than in northern Portugal.

FACT FILE

Region: Planícies (Alentejo).

Provinces: Alentejo (Alto and Baixo).

Main towns and cities: Évora, Beja, Elvas, Vila Viçosa, Portalegre, Estremoz, Moura, Sines.

Industry/Economy: cork, olives, cereal, marble, wine, carpets and rugs, ceramics.

Typical food and drink: pork with clams, Elvas sugar plums, wine, cheeses, rabbit, kid and lamb stews.

Things to do and see: Évora world heritage city, Elvas aqueduct and fortifications, megalithic sites, Marvão castle and spectacular views, Bragança palace and estate at Vila Viçosa, untouched beaches down Atlantic coast.

Transport links: few rail links, buses and coaches run between most places, but not always at convenient times, IP7, IP8 and IP2 highways cross the region, and many major roads are in reasonable condition.

Types of property: white-washed rustic cottages, more modern apartments in town centres, larger 70s and 80s houses on town outskirts, some with gardens.

Prices: small country cottages from €40,000/farmhouses with outbuildings, some needing restoration, €80-100,000+/larger country houses from €700,000.

Info: Região de Turismo de Évora, Rua de Aviz, 90, 7000-591 Évora. Plus Directory.

THE ALGARVE

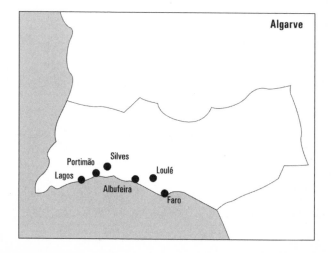

The **Algarve**, so named by its Moorish invaders **Al Gharb** (the west), is not as totally given over to tourism as the mention of its name in brochures suggests. The holiday complexes dominate the coast for a thin strip, stretching across approximately 4/5 of the region. The far eastern and western parts remain largely untouched and are areas of outstanding beauty, with important nature reserves. The coast of the western Algarve particularly, is a wild Atlantic environment, with ideal walking areas. Houses are mostly white, and vestiges of both Moorish and Roman occupation can be seen in architecture (flat roof-top terraces), water irrigation channels, citrus fruits and *amêndoas* (almonds), and place names (al = Arabic for 'the') eg, **Alcoutim**. Many people are employed in the intense tourist trade, and work alongside foreign residents in for example real estate, entertainment and car-hire. The main holiday factors here are the high number of hours of sunshine, beautiful, safe and clean beaches, spectacular rocky cliff-tops, and easy direct access to the main airport, **Faro**, recently upgraded and extended. But the Algarve is not simply about holidays. From about 6 km in from the coast the landscape emerges without constriction of the villa complexes as wonderfully wild, protected by the high ridge of the **Monchique hills**. The pace of life is languid, hot in the summer, and sometimes uncomfortably damp in the winter as few houses are set up with adequate heating.

FACT FILE

Region: Algarve.

Provinces: Algarve.

Main towns and cities: Faro, Portimão, Lagos, Silves, Albufeira, Loulé,

Olhão, Tavira.

Industry/Economy: tourism, ceramics, weaving, salt, wine, cork production, some fishing, small scale farming.

Typical food and drink: seafood and fish, especially grilled sardines, piri-piri chicken, almond sweets, citrus fruits.

Things to do and see: spa and woodlands in Monchique, great beaches, nature reserves, Sagres and Cape St. Vincent, Moorish castle in Silves, Loulé market.

Transport links: Faro airport; trains along the coast, although many stations are some way outside the towns, link to north at Tunes; IP1 highway links across the Algarve to Spain, relieving the old EN125 road; frequent bus and coach services.

Types of property: modern luxurious villas, apartments, holiday complexes, some older, typical rustic houses, golf resort property.

Prices: depends very much on location – pricey in centre and golfing vicinities and resorts, eg. Quinta do Lago and Vilamoura. Apartments from €200-900,000. Villas now easily from €500,000 up to €2 million. Elsewhere, apartments range from €80,000 upwards, and town houses and villas €140,000+. Prices are being pushed up by a steady stream of purchasers, including sports stars and personalities, and the reputation of the standard of facilities on the complexes.

Info: Região de Turismo do Algarve, Av.5 de Outubro, 18, Apartado 106, 8001-902 Faro. Plus Directory.

MADEIRA AND THE AÇORES

Built on volcanic outcrops, and each home to about ¼ million people, these two groups of islands are autonomous regions of Portugal. Madeira has long-since been a popular holiday destination of the British particularly, who enjoy its quiet splendour, especially in Spring when the island blooms with a myriad of colourful flowers. Walkers take advantage of the challenging routes up the '*levadas*' (irrigation channels), and others simply sit back and accept the pampering in some of the elegant top hotels, such as the world-renowned Reids. Madeira produces the famous dessert wine, bananas and exquisite hand-made embroidery. The Açores, named after the hawks (*açor*) seen circling the island by explorers, probably attract fewer mainstream visitors, being more untamed in nature, but offer a unique experience of local living. Tours have become popular for whale watching, an eco-tourism project developed from the traditional life-style of whale-hunting. Some towns have been awarded UNESCO world heritage status, eg. **Angra do Heroísmo**, as important sites of architectural and cultural interest. Many families from the islands move to Jersey and the Channel Islands to work in the hotel industry, as this offers opportunities for a better quality of life.

FACT FILE

Region: Madeira and the Açores.

Main towns and cities: Funchal, Monte, Machico, Santana, Ribeira Brava, Câmara dos Lobos; islands of São Miguel, Terceira, São Jorge, Pico, Faial.

Industry/Economy: tourism, wine, bananas, flowers, fishing, lace, embroidery and wicker work, leather goods.

Typical food and drink: sword fish, fish with bananas, sweet dessert wine, fruits, pineapple, honey cake, kebab-style meat, casseroles, pork dishes.

Things to do and see: walk the levadas, whale-watching, flower festival, Funchal cathedral, Botanical Gardens, traditional toboggan ride down the slopes; Holy Spirit festivals, rugged landscapes.

Transport links: Madeira airport; buses link main towns; car hire available but routes can be frighteningly high and twisting; flights or ferry boats to nearby islands; airports link the Azorean islands; ferries link all islands; buses run to local destinations; car hire and taxis more convenient.

Types of property: rustic – typical Madeiran houses have sloping roofs, basic cottages, some luxurious villas, town-centre flats.

Prices: Madeira – cottages €80,000+/ apartments from €150,000. Modern houses and larger apartments from €200,000 to €1 million +. Azores – apartments from €100,000/ rustic cottages from €30,000 and houses with land from €75,000.

Info: Direcção Regional do Turismo, Avenida Arriaga, 18, 9004-519 Funchal/ Direcção Regional do Turismo, Rua Comendador Ernesto Rebelo, 14, 9900-501 Horta, Faial. Plus Directory.

HOUSE VALUES SURVEY

A survey carried out in 2003, by the Estate Agents Association (APEMI) in Portugal, gave the following values per square metre for detached houses in Portugal:

Lisbon	€1569
Lisbon coast	€1109
south of Tagus	€858
Albufeira/Praia de Rocha/Carvoeiro/Vilamoura	€996
Lagos/Portimão/Faro/Quarteira	€878
Silves/Lagoa/Loulé/Tavira	€783

SUMMARY

Even with such a brief overview of Portugal's regions, I am sure you can see that this small country indeed has a great variety of locations to consider. Although it is easier to get to the Algarve on cheap flights, it is really worth having a look elsewhere too, before you make a decision – you may be surprised at how much more you can get for your money, and how much more to life there is beyond the Irish pub and English breakfast enclaves of parts of the southern coast. Arm yourself with more information by investing in good guide books such as the Dorling Kindersley books, Rough Guide, or those with maps, such as the AA guides, and read as much as you can about Portugal whilst you are still in the planning stage. For more suggestions of books, contacts and email sites, see the Directory at the end of the book.

3

What to Buy

WHERE DO THE PORTUGUESE LIVE?

The style of Portuguese domestic architecture varies from north to south, and from the cities to the rural regions: from humble, stone and slate-built dwellings, to apartments in old city-centre buildings, or modern flats and houses. Some Portuguese still live in pretty poor conditions, whilst others live in style in luxurious villas or manor houses. The whole gamut of accommodation is represented.

Wherever the Portuguese live these days, the vast majority now benefit from electricity and piped water (although for some these have only come in the past couple of decades). Piped gas is still relatively rare; the majority of households rely on bottled gas (*garrafas de gás*) for all their needs. Ownership of domestic appliances has risen steadily over the last decade: in 1998 97% of households had a fridge, compared with 94% at the start of the decade, washing-machine ownership went up from 68% to 85% over the same period. Fewer houses possess a freezer (55%), dish-washer (15%) or microwave (15%). Most residences, though, have the all-important window shutters (either wooden, or the pull-down metal type), the first line in defence against the elements of both summer and winter.

WHERE DO FOREIGNERS LIVE?

The vast majority of foreign visitors and residents buy or rent in the Algarve (75% of all purchases on the southern coast are by Brits), and a glance in the property section of any of the main English papers (especially week-end editions, see Chapter 4), serves to illustrate that in the main people tend towards modern apartments and villas. Along with the Dutch and Germans, the English have created their very own enclaves along the southern coast, with a host of English-oriented activities to make themselves feel at home. These include weekly whist and bridge meetings, car-boot sales and charity events, drama groups and a fair sprinkling of alcoholic-support groups! For more on enjoying life in Portugal, see Chapter 14.

Demand has started to outstrip supply in the Algarve, and despite the large number of developments still coming along, prices have really taken a hike in the last couple of years. People who bought as recently as a couple of years ago will, by now, have seen a hefty increase in the value of their property. Chapter 10, however, outlines the new Portuguese property tax regulations, which will affect numerous people who bought via an off-shore company, and which may see a number of people having to find an awful lot of money in back-payments.

Some people do venture outside the safety realm of ex-patriot communities, and renovate old farm buildings, or buy plots of land and have property built to their own specifications. You can even do this a few miles inland off the Algarve coast, and be in wild countryside, whilst maintaining a quick link to beaches and larger shopping locations. The price difference can be stunning. One couple interviewed said that had they bought their current house a few miles south of the main EN125 highway, rather than to the north, where it actually is, they would have paid three times more for it.

A number of foreign visitors stay (often renting) in areas around Lisbon, Oporto and Coimbra, usually for business purposes, or whilst studying or teaching. New, exclusive complexes have been developed in the Lisbon-Sintra-Coastal areas, and not only aimed at foreign investors. Adverts in Portuguese newspaper supplements extol the virtues of modern, luxury living within commuter distances of the capital. As for the more rural areas of central and northern Portugal, and the northern coast-lines, it is quite rare to find foreign property-owners, although there are a few dotted about.

TYPES OF HOUSES
A typical Portuguese town does not look like its equivalent in the UK, as far more people live in flats, often above shops, and many in old buildings, some of

which look quite neglected. However, the outskirts of towns often have a mix of detached houses with their own gardens, and modern apartment blocks. There is frequently a feel of the old mingling with the new, a state which may be said of Portugal on the whole, as it embraces the new technological era, whilst holding on proudly to its links with its great heritage.

House types may include:

apartamento	apartment/flat
parcela/terreno/lote	land/plot
estúdio	studio flat
celeiro	barn
apartamento conjugado	studio
casa modelo	show house
bloco/prédio	block of flats
casa de férias	holiday house
condomínio (fechado)	(security) complex/estate
casa de praia	beach house
aldeia turística/ *aldeiamento turístico*	holiday village
casa rústica	rustic house
urbanização	development/estate
casa de campo	rustic house
moradia (isolada)	detached house
moinho	windmill
moradia geminada	semi-detached house
quinta	farm
casas contíguas/geminadas	terraced
solar	manor
vivenda/ vila	villa
'duplex'	maisonette

LIVING IN SMALL VILLAGES

In rural areas most people live in small, basic houses which may be a terrace-style in the town centre, or detached cottages and farm-houses. Dwellings are likely to be old, with few facilities, although the women of households in the Alentejo and Algarve take pride in their regular white-washing of the exterior walls, to such an extent that in some areas it brings out a real competitive streak! Bright exteriors, meanwhile, often mask the reality many people in Portugal live with – no central heating, humidity and damp, and for some there are still no inside toilets (in the Alentejo, for example, this is true for approximately 20% of households). In the winters, which can be harsh, families often sit around a table whose tablecloth hides an electric fire underneath. The '*braseira*' is a common feature of many homes; you place your feet and legs under the cloth and warm yourself at meal-times. There may be open fires, and heavy shutters at the windows, but little else to keep out the cold. Women often wear thick *xailes*, and lots of jumpers indoors, and people sleep under many layers of blankets, with the typical hand-woven wool rugs (*colchas de tear*) on top. The lack of adequate heating and, in many cases, ventilation, means that most Portuguese houses also have a problem with damp - the majority of bathrooms never eradicate the black mildew from the walls and ceiling.

In smaller places, people tend to know each other well, which can have its pros and cons. There is a well-developed sense of community, typically manifested through town/village festivals and traditions. Sources of entertainment are more limited, and may focus on local bars and cafes, with some smaller-scale cultural features, such as cinema, musical events and dances.

LIVING IN THE CITIES

In larger towns and cities housing can be much more modern, apart from the old city centres themselves, where families still live in traditional apartments in old, brooding-looking buildings. Living conditions can be cramped (extended family and students may typically live at home), and the buildings often suffer from a lack of maintenance. This is due in the main to the fact that by law rents have traditionally been fixed for life; subsequently landlords have found it economically unfeasible to look after their properties. A walk around Lisbon, for example, will illustrate the number of once-elegant buildings in shady tree-lined avenues, with flaking façades and dingy interiors. Some underwent face-lifts in an attempt to spruce up the capital for the 1998 Expo, but much still remains to be done.

Rental prices in Lisbon and Oporto, for families wishing to move, are now so exorbitant that most people simply stay put and endure the conditions around them. On the outskirts (*os arredores*) of the cities, and the urban sprawl of many larger towns in the countryside, most people live in modern housing, almost 70% of which has been built since 1960. The 70s were a boom decade for housing – mostly apartment blocks – and even today around 70,000 new buildings are constructed each year. Around 40% of the population live in an apartment of some description – be it in a small block in a country town, or one of the high-rise council flats outside Lisbon or Oporto.

Although council rents are low, some of these estates suffer the same problems as elsewhere in the world – a conglomeration of the most needy, isolation from each other, lack of facilities, decay and deprivation. One step beyond are the outlying shanty towns, (*bairros de lata*) corrugated huts mostly inhabited by gypsies and immigrants.

Larger towns offer a wider range of things to do, and it is easier to assume a faceless identity, if that is what you prefer. There are fewer large cities in Portugal than in the UK, with only Lisbon proper and Oporto claiming approximately 1 million inhabitants. Larger places also come encumbered by their own problems, such as traffic and parking, hustle and bustle (which, of course, you may actually enjoy), and higher incidences of crime (Lisbon as a capital city has seen an increase in crime rates in recent years, largely due to drug-related attacks). However, a flurry of articles in the Portuguese press about the dangers lurking on Lisbon's streets, it is still very true to say that Portugal, and Lisbon itself, is a relatively safe place to visit. Certainly I have never felt unease there, even whilst a single young woman out at night.

LIVING IN HOLIDAY VILLAGE COMPLEXES

Holiday villages, golfing developments and private estates are designed in the main, for short stays, although many people decide to buy on a complex and use either for frequent visits, or longer-term. Many developments are now being marketed for investment purposes (see also Chapter 8, on buy-to-let). In the Lisbon area and parts of the Algarve particularly, luxury private estates are aimed at the discerning (and wealthy) foreigners and Portuguese alike, for high-class modern living. The **Ria Formosa** national park in the Algarve is home to the upmarket **Quinta do Lago** development, with an extensive British community in residence there. See the website: *www.quintadolago.net* for details. Other popular estates and resorts include **Parque da Floresta** golf and leisure resort, an award-winning development, where town houses will set you back at least £200,000; **Quinta de São Roque** near Lagos – see: *www.saoroque.com*; **Campo Real Golfe** and **Natureza** just north of Lisbon, and within reach of some wonderful beaches. Here you have a golf course, health club/spa, tennis, equestrian centre and exclusive apartments and townhouses from around £198,000 upwards (info from tel: 020-8940-9406 Premier Resorts Limited).

The pros of such locations are:
♦ modern property with many mod-cons
♦ on-site facilities, such as shops, bars, restaurants, pool and entertainment
♦ management services
♦ pool cleaning and other domestic services
♦ constant contact with other visitors/ residents
♦ security – often gated
♦ status symbol
♦ proximity to golf facilities.

The cons to consider may be:
♦ property lacks character – 'all made out of ticky-tacky and they all look just the same'
♦ no need to ever venture outside the enclosure and see some of Portugal

- prices may be holiday-hiked
- number of extra charges for year-round maintenance
- little or no contact with 'the natives'
- little chance to use the language
- getting on with close neighbours/nuisances, especially in peak holiday times
- community rules and regulations.

There are now a few so-called 'retirement' villages, such as that at **Monte da Palhagueira**, **Santa Bárbara de Nexe**, near Faro. This particular one lists apartments from £80,000, built in small blocks, fully kitted, with gardens and parking. They sell on the basis of a lifetime occupancy contract. They can be contacted via Clive Roberts, email: *monte.palhagueira@netc.pt*.

COAST OR INLAND – LOCATION, LOCATION, LOCATION

The Algarve's housing is a blend representing its tourist trappings. Whilst the Portuguese there live in mostly typical old houses or more recent flats, the high-rise luxury holiday apartments and villa complexes mushroomed out of control during the 80s. It looked as though Portugal was going the same way as Spain's Costas, until the PROTAL law of the early 90s declared that no more new massive construction could be undertaken on land that did not have prior building consent. This curbed expansion to a certain extent, but not totally. Some development has been allowed on protected green areas and the building sites, cranes and placards are a constant reminder of the increasing number of people who wish to visit this region. The exclusive villas are mostly holiday or second homes of foreign visitors or residents, as a glance at the name-plates will reveal.

The northern coastlines are virtually untapped resources of beauty and serenity and are much more quintessentially Portuguese. They can easily be reached by rail from Lisbon all the way to the border with Spain, by flight to either Lisbon or Oporto, or by car, entering from northern Spain (Galicia), via the ferry crossings to Santander or Bilbao.

As most people are usually drawn to buying in Portugal as a result of glorious holidays there, it is more often the case that they will end up on the coast, with access to beaches and tourist facilities. However, for those who are just as happy without sand, sea and sangria, Portugal's countryside offers calm, rural retreats, integration into the Portuguese way of life, cheaper prices, and opportunities for more natural pursuits or business openings connected to quality or 'green' tourism. City life can also be very rewarding in Portugal, with a number of cultural activities, the buzz of a more vibrant atmosphere, and a wider choice of places to eat, shop and see and be seen (although, apart from Lisbon and Oporto, many larger towns in Portugal may still have a more limited choice than in many UK towns).

Let us consider the advantages and disadvantages of all three types of location:

Coast
Advantages
Close to beach life, vibrant in tourist areas, good facilities – food etc.

Disadvantages

Too noisy, higher prices, too many tourists, not the real Portugal (in the south), less to do in winter and beaches packed in summer.

Inland
Advantages

Cheaper, rural idyll, more typical life, safe, privacy, larger plots of land.

Disadvantages

Not such good transport links, extremes of climate, isolation, lack of facilities, fewer neighbours, may lack amenities, such as water or electricity etc.

Cities
Advantages

Lots to do, more facilities, good transport links.

Disadvantages

Higher prices, noise and bustle, rising crime, very hot in summer.

NEW HOUSE OR RESALE?

The majority of people buy new properties, many going for off-plan purchases, where all they may see beforehand is a model of the proposed property and its plans. If you go down this route, be sure to ask to see examples of other developments completed by the same company, and check the standard of finish. Some real estate agents only recommend this type of purchase as financial investment, and not as a way of buying your own property. Brand new properties certainly have their appeal in terms of how they are kitted out and the facilities they come furnished with, but resale homes (whether just a few years old, or a hundred) also have appeal. It is worth considering the pros and cons of all.

New home
Advantages
Includes fixtures and fittings, brand new décor and finish, ready to move into, good re-let potential, good amenities – often have/near pool etc.

Disadvantages
Little character – all the same, sterile interior, often lack personal outdoor space.

Off-plan
Advantages
Can be done to your own specifications, up-to-date, good return on investment.

Disadvantages
Have to wait to complete, have to visualise it and may not turn out as planned, have to pay money up front and potential for companies to go bust, can be subject to legal/planning disputes.

Resale
Advantages
Lived-in feel, can see any on-going problems, older properties have real character and house has a history.

Disadvantages
Quality of some more recent building not great, not your own feel, may require work, possibly outdated facilities.

ACCESS AND FACILITIES

Wherever you are looking around for a home, in addition to the property itself, there are various factors you should take into account in order to avoid future problems and unhappiness. Here are some points to consider:

- ◆ Position
  - – Is it facing the sun?
  - – Is there a good amount of shade for summer?
  - – Is there shelter from the rain?
  - – Are there steep slopes? This is especially important if you have children.
  - – What is the security like? Are walls/gates needed? Where are the nearest neighbours?
  - – is the town centre noisy – especially at night?
  - – What about traffic noise? How close is the property to the vicinity of motorways or airport flight paths?

- ◆ Access to the property
  - – Is it up a rough track or steep hill?
  - – What will the road conditions be like in winter or rain?
  - – Consider the type of vehicle you may need.
  - – What will it be like for carrying shopping or to get your belongings there?
  - – Are the parking facilities adequate?

- ◆ Transport/communication links
  - – Is there a frequent bus or rail service?
  - – What are the travel times from airports?
  - – Is there a good postal or delivery service?

- If there is no existing telephone, how long before service can be supplied?
- How close are your nearest neighbours in case of problems?
- Are there schools, health clinic and shops in the vicinity?
- How far is the nearest form of entertainment?

SPOTTING POTENTIAL PROBLEMS

Whether you are buying old or new, apartment or farmhouse, for a pittance or a fortune, a good eye for possible defects or potential problems may just save you from sinking your money into a bottomless pit. Don't rely entirely on anyone else in the official process to point things out to you. Inspect the property yourself, ideally in both winter and summer, look in every nook and cranny, and be prepared to ask awkward questions if necessary. Think like a surveyor might. Here are some ideas for things to scrutinise, and tell-tale signs to look out for:

- Quality of stonework.

- Artificial stone facade may cover poor work behind.

- Poor porous bricks may allow dampness to penetrate.

- Is there a damp course? – Ask for evidence.

- Are the floors stone or wood? If wood, is there ventilation below them?

- Soft or flaky plasterwork suggests it has perished.

- Cracks in walls are evidence of underlying problems.

- Observe floors in general, for woodworm, dry or wet rot.

- Check roof space for wood problems.

- Check the state of the roof.

- Powdery slates suggest possibility of subsidence.

- Are gutters and pipes working properly?

- Is drainage mains sewerage or septic tank?

- What shared services and maintenance are there?

- What is standard of drinking water? Tank water could be stale or contaminated.

- Foundations – check general state of local ground or neighbour's property.

- Cracked or crazed cement rendering, pointing to brickwork or around windows suggests problems.

- Excess of wet or dryness in ground can both give problems.

- Check access to roads and paths, e.g. ownership/ upkeep.

- Is gas mains supply or portable?

- Is the electric supply mains or generator?

- Look out for local water courses or dikes, and especially any with tidal influence.

- Check future building plans – both local and national (see also Chapter 9).

◆ Flat roofs are always potentially a problem for rain penetration (and yes, it does rain in the Algarve!)

SUMMARY

Although it is a good idea to be thinking about the type of place and property you would be happy in, it is also worthwhile keeping an open mind. Visit as many different locations and types of properties as you can, especially at varying times of the year. What seems idyllic in the haze of the summer sun may well be a wet and wind-swept nightmare in the winter. Devise a checklist – both a personal wish-list and a list of vital points to verify. Ask lots of questions and *don't* be fobbed off by half-hearted answers. If you are not satisfied, look elsewhere. Talk to potential neighbours and other people living or working around the area. Don't put pen to paper in the process until you are absolutely sure you have found the right place – it could prove costly in more ways than one.

Glossary

See also Chapter 4 on interpreting a Portuguese advert.

sun	*sol*
bus/rail frequency	*frequência dos autocarros/ comboios*
shade	*sombra*
distance – airport	*distância – aeroporto*
shelter	*abrigo*
postal service	*serviço dos correios*
rain	*chuva*
telephone	*telefone*
slopes – steep	*encostas escarpadas*

school/shops	*escola/lojas*
security – wall/gate	*segurança – muro/portão*
health clinic	*posto de saúde*
neighbours	*vizinhos*
entertainment	*atracções/diversões*
road/track	*estrada/caminho*
damp course	*impermeabilização*
access	*aceso*
wood – floor	*madeira/chão*
gas	*gás*
woodworm	*carcoma*
electricity	*electricidade/luz*
dry rot	*apodrecimento seco*
(drinking) water	*água (potável)*
wet rot	*putrefacção fungosa*
drains	*esgotos*
septic tank	*fossa (séptica)*
roof	*telhado*
basement	*cave*
attic	*sótão*
kitchen	*cozinha*
bathroom	*casa de banho*
loo	*retrete/casa de banho*
dining room	*sala de jantar*
living room/lounge	*sala de estar*
bedroom	*quarto*
pool	*piscina*
terrace	*terraço*
garden	*jardim*
garage	*garagem*

4

Finding Your Property

People find property through a variety of tried and tested ways, often using a combination of more than one method. It is certainly worth considering the different options and keeping an open mind about the process.

NEWSPAPERS
There are three main journalistic sources of house information: UK newspapers, English-speaking papers in Portugal, and Portuguese newspapers, as well as specialist overseas property magazines, although the vast majority of these focus on Spain and France.

In the UK, most daily papers have overseas property sections, but the main listings come out in the weekend editions. Papers like the *Telegraph*, *Times*, *Daily Mail* and others have property supplements, quite often with key articles about purchasing/life in featured countries, plus a wide selection of adverts from private vendors and agencies alike. *The Sunday Times* runs a particularly good supplement. Even if the articles are about countries other than Portugal, they are usually worth reading, as they throw light on the whole area of buying and living overseas, and may give valuable insights into what you may be about to embark on. Many of the houses advertised through these means tend to be the more modern villas and apartments, although you do also see the odd ad or two for older, rural buildings.

In Portugal, the main English-speaking publications *The Anglo-Portuguese News (APN)*, *Algarve Resident,* and *The News* carry adverts and features on local property sales. The *News*, in particular, has a separate property section, which, in addition to the published paper, can also be accessed via its website (see Directory section). It can be contacted by email too, on: *property@the-news.net* Properties featured are mostly in the Algarve, although there are a good number in the Lisbon area too. There are also local businesses for sale, such as bars and restaurants, often with accommodation attached. If you have friends in Portugal, you could ask them to send you copies of the papers, otherwise you can subscribe to them from the UK: details in Directory on p 219.

Madeira also has its own monthly paper, *The Madeira Island Bulletin,* available from: Apartado 621, 9001-907 Funchal, Madeira.

In Portugal, the local, regional, and national papers all have property ads, usually in the section marked *classificados*, or *anúncios*. Look for the columns headed *imobiliário* (property), *vende-se* (for sale) or *aluga-se/arrenda-se* (to rent). The main papers to check out are: *O Público, Diário de Notícias, Correio da Manhã*, and *Jornal de Notícias,* as well as the many regional and local publications. The main papers are also available on the internet:

www.publico.pt
www.dn.pt
www.correiomanha.pt
www.jn.pt

The Directory has many more sites for you to explore.

For guidance on understanding Portuguese adverts see page 56.

Specialist magazines dealing with overseas property have mushroomed in the last few years, at the same pace as the TV programmes extolling the virtues of a move abroad. There are some very good ones aimed at Spain and France, which are sometimes worth a glance, as they have very good articles about cultural integration or potential pitfalls, both of which are applicable to any country. A useful one I have found which also features Portugal is *Homes Overseas (The International Homefinder)*. It is published in association with an overseas exhibition company, and has many adverts from estate agents, financial organisations, and relocation companies.

Although the material on Portugal itself is minimal, the magazine, which comes out monthly, is an interesting font of general information. It can be bought at WHSmiths and other large newsagents, and has its own website: *www.homesoverseas.co.uk*. There are also snippets in other, similar magazines, such as *World of Property, Private Villas, Dalton's Weekly*. *The Algarve Golf Guide* also has houses (mostly villas) for sale.

In Portugal, Vista Ibérica Publicações Lda publishes a bi-monthly magazine called *Algarve Property Advertiser*, which again includes a combination of articles and ads. They can be contacted by email at: *vista.lda@netvisao.pt*. Their publications are also distributed in the UK, and you should be able to get hold of them via a good newsagent.

International property consultants David Headland Associates publish their own guide, which includes hundreds of properties. It is called *The Ultimate Property Guide (Algarve)* and is available by calling 01933-353333. Or to view properties, try their website: *www.headlands. co.uk*. From 2000 to 2002 they were voted 'Best Portuguese Estate Agent' (in the UK), and have over 30 years' experience in selling in Portugal, so are a safe bet when it comes to requesting advice.

PROPERTY EXHIBITIONS
Most exhibitions in the UK tend to focus on Spain, although some do have stands representing Portuguese companies and agents. They are predominantly of new properties, and tend to be held in large hotels and conference centres in larger cities around the UK. Ads for

them run in the main press, and the organisers have their own websites for information. Here are a few to start you off:

www.outboundpublishing.com
www.internationalpropertyshow.com
www.homesoverseas.co.uk
www.homebuyer.co.uk
www.worldclasshomes.co.uk

View exhibitions as another means of information-gathering; an opportunity to get brochures, contact details and have a chat to reps about the buying process, and the types of properties their companies have on their books. Ask questions, but don't feel pressurised into signing up to anything at this stage. Although, undoubtedly, reps will be wanting to capture people's interest and trying to sign them onto inspection flights to view houses, it is not to your benefit to commit yourself amidst all the heat and bustle invariably associated with exhibitions.

ESTATE AGENTS

In the south of Portugal there are so many British (and some German/Dutch) estate agents (*mediador autorizado/imobiliário*), the choice is rather bewildering, and whilst there are some Portuguese agents too, the array of English-speaking agencies is decidedly overpowering. The showrooms are like those in the UK, and the range of services they offer tends to cover sales, purchase or rental of property, plus letting and management. Some of the more experienced agents can also offer guidance and contacts for the financial side of the process, plus conveyancing services. Fees to the agent are only paid by the vendor, at about 5% of asking price, plus IVA (VAT).

All legally-operating agents (whether foreign or Portuguese) in Portugal must be government registered, and have an official AMI (*Associação de Mediadores Imobiliários*) number displayed. Ask to see one.

The UK Portuguese Chamber of Commerce, in London, has a website with a list of licensed agents: *www.imoppi.pt.* On the right-hand menu click on '*mediação imobiliária*'. On the left-hand menu click on '*empresas licenciadas*'. Click on '*por região*' and then you can click on the map of Portugal any areas of interest. The search will bring up companies in that area; click '*sim*' (yes) to see their details. The Chamber can supply details of the companies' telephone/fax/email, on request. Contact them either by telephone on 020-7494-1844, or by email at *info@portuguese-chamber.org.uk*.

In Portugal AFPOP, the Foreign Property Owners Association also has a list of AMI members, and in the UK, reputable agents should be members of the Federation of Overseas Property Developers, Agents and Consultants.

PORTUGUESE ESTATE AGENTS

Away from the south, you will be dealing almost exclusively with Portuguese estate agents who will have varying levels of English. Some will have a good knowledge of English or French, others less so. It will be even more vital for you to have a working knowledge of Portuguese, or have someone with you who can help out, to avoid possible lapses in communication which could ultimately prove costly. Apart from this, the process involved is the same as anywhere, except agents may not be as pro-active as you might otherwise be used to. The range of properties, plans and photos on display may be quite small and you may have to push to get things rolling. There is often more inside the shop but, according to one purchaser who bought in central Portugal, 'you would not know they were for sale unless you ask! Don't just look in the window'.

However, positive comments on using estate agents are clear from most people you speak to:

> 'Our experience with estate agents has been very good. Most of the work is done by the lawyer so your own contact with Portuguese officials is minimal. Once we had selected a property, the estate agent helped us through the process.'

> 'We used a local estate agent to form a short list of six properties. We then viewed them and reduced the short list to two. We also used estate agents' websites to get info on the buying process.'

UK AGENTS

In the UK there are some agents who are specialists in Portuguese property. Some also offer advice on the purchase process, and can guide you towards the financial aspects too. Some of the main ones dealing with Portugal include:

David Headland Associates
Quinta da Arrábida SA
Noblelink Limited
Prime Property International
Cerro Novo Lda
Quadrant Overseas Property Ltd.

See also Directory.

Many companies simply act as agents for their Portuguese counterparts, introducing customers to them. Whilst it may be very useful to have an English-speaking, UK-based representative to deal with, you may be charged a hefty commission for the service. Check in advance what the fees are likely to be and what these cover, then, if you can, compare this with what you might pay should you go direct with someone based in Portugal. The difference may be surprising, and may warrant a trip to Portugal and the search for someone to act for you over there.

USING THE INTERNET

For a general overview of the buying process in Portugal, you can check out the BBC site: BBC/ NEWS/ Working lunch, which ran a series on buying abroad. A useful site with articles on the process, plus pictures of houses for sale is the overseas property search site: *www.newskys.co.uk*.

A Portuguese site offering information in different regions is: *www.imoregioes.com*.

Many property companies also have their own websites, which you will find in their ads. The Directory on page 219 gives you some more to explore, although no guarantee can be given that any of the sites listed at the time of writing are still 'live'. However, you can also search yourself, by typing in Portugal + property.

Ads on the net can be placed by companies or private individuals. They are useful as an extra means of information-gathering. Many have beautiful pictures of the properties offered. As with many aspects of the internet, be cautious when giving out any of your own personal details. You will still need to be in Portugal to see the places for yourself, so you need to check how *bona fide* the advert is (is there a phone number to talk to someone direct?), what are the arrangements for visiting, what can they send you via the post?

UNDERSTANDING ADVERTS

If you are considering scouring the Portuguese press or internet sites for adverts, the following may be useful in interpreting the language used.

imobiliário	estate agent
propriedade	property
apartamento	apartment/flat
moradia	house
vende-se	for sale
aluga-se	to let
trespassa-se	to lease
terreno	land
com garagem	with garage

arrenda-se	to let
mobilado	furnished
remodelado	refurbished
novo	new
bem localizado	good location
nos arredores	on outskirts
usado	used
frente à praia	opposite beach
vista panorâmica	panoramic view
lote	plot
andar/piso	floor/storey
T1/2/3 etc	number bedrooms
vivenda	villa
prédio	building
aparcamento	parking
(sem) mobília	(without) furniture
para férias	for holidays
perto de...	near
equipado	equipped
quinta	farm
em construção	under construction
aquecimento (central)	(central) heating
urbanização	complex/estate
vidros duplos	double glazing
porta de segurança	security door
bons acabamentos	good finish
local tranquilo	peaceful location
vistas sobre a cidade/o campo/o mar	views of city/countryside/sea
pronto a habitar	ready to move in
casa de praia	beach house
condomínio (fechado)	(closed) complex

preço negociável	price negotiable
venda urgente	urgent sale
x divisões	X rooms

PRIVATE SALES

Vende-se (for sale) is often painted on the side of buildings, or on home-made signs, along with a telephone number. If your Portuguese is good enough, you may be able to strike up a good deal direct with the vendors. If not, you will need someone, such as your appointed lawyer, to negotiate for you. You will, in any case, still need to employ all the necessary people to carry out the process for you. See Chapter 6.

Amongst the ex-patriot communities, or even just within the circles of frequent visitors, word goes round of residents with a property to sell, and often this is a very good starting point. It can also lead to other, useful contacts, such as for agents or builders, and save you a lot of time, effort and money into the bargain. It is worth talking to foreign residents in bars and cafes to see what they know. Barbara Baird, from Manchester told me that

> *'Friends who had gone through the same process were able to direct us to a solicitor, who in turn directed us to an engineer. They also found us a Portuguese builder and told us where the best supermarkets, builders merchants could be found.'*

Another couple I interviewed had the following to say:

'We'd met some people who invited us for coffee one evening – it was dark. A couple of years later my husband decided to try to find their house in daylight. He did and as we went round the bend, there was this incredible view. There was a field for sale so we stopped to ask a lady the price (she was English and there were only three houses there). She told us that one of the houses was for sale. We weren't seriously looking at the time, but we bought it eventually. It's fantastic!'

AUCTIONS

Auctions are advertised in the Portuguese papers. They operate in the same way as they do in the UK, but you do need to do a lot of preliminary research on the condition of the property, estimates for work, and legal status of the building. It is essential that you have legal representation for the auction, and have everything in place for the process, should you strike lucky. Bargains can be had, but it would certainly be unwise to try to go through these means without sound Portuguese backing.

VIEWING PROPERTY

Unless you are buying something off-plan (in which case you should at least be able to look at the detailed plans, site and a model of the proposed building), arrangements to view property can be made through the vendor's agent, the estate agent, or with the vendors themselves. It is somewhat difficult to say which is the most beneficial:

Through the agent

The agent will give you the 'guided tour', interspersed with agent commentary. They will usually want to show you the best features and highlight the positive aspects.

Remember they have a financial interest in selling the property. However, as a third party presence, it can often be easier to ask more awkward questions of them and have a better look around.

House owner/vendor

With the vendor showing you the property it may be more difficult to have a good nose around as you may feel embarrassed and less inclined to discuss critical points. It's useful, though, to get their low-down on life in the locality. Hopefully they will be realistic and honest in their responses, but always be prepared to follow up by exploring further yourself.

If you find a property you are interested in, you will probably benefit from more than one viewing. In the interest of a successful sale, it should not matter to all parties how many times you request to see the place, although patience may wear thin if you start dithering. Ultimately you may lose out on the sale yourself if there are other interested parties on the same trail.

If you are looking for property through a UK-based agency, you may be offered an inspection flight at a discount rate. Usually these last around three days, and you are accompanied the whole time, shown various properties, and not given the chance to do your own thing. They are obviously looking for a sale at the end of it all, and it can be a very tiring way of checking what there is in a fairly limited location. You may be better off in the long-run taking a cheap flight over yourself and taking time to look around at leisure.

SUMMARY

Use as many sources as you can whilst you are in the research stage. Amass as much information as you can about different locations, types of house, local life and prices. Read up about the whole process, and also about Portugal itself (see also Chapter 11), so you are more prepared to integrate there. When you start to get down to the nitty-gritty of looking at houses, make sure you check agents out for official licences. Always get a written run-down of fees and make sure there are no hidden costs so that you can make realistic comparisons between agencies. With any form of information, make sure you have the whole picture before you start making decisions. Once you do, there is no reason to believe that the process will not progress to its ultimate, happy, conclusion, as it has for many thousands of people before you.

5

Renting Whilst You Look

WHY RENT?

Not everybody is in an immediate position to purchase property. You may well have taken the decision to move to Portugal, and may possibly be imminently homeless if you have sold or rented out your own house in the UK. You may be sent to work in Portugal, or wish to move there to try your luck in the marketplace before settling on a more permanent basis. In any case, even if you are desperate to buy something, it is very worthwhile visiting on a number of occasions to check out locations and conditions at different times of the year.

There are various options for short-to-medium stays, from guest houses, to local lets, and in the Algarve, the more typical holiday let, which can be from a couple of weeks to a few months. Your location will dictate what there is on offer, and to what degree you will need a working knowledge of the language in order to sign up to rental agreements. In the Algarve, for example, you will be able to get by with very little Portuguese, even for many of the private lets, whereas in the north or central regions, you may struggle to understand what is being offered and what are your rights and responsibilities. Having said that, on the whole, if you go through an estate agent, you will usually find someone who can speak English.

It is worth thinking about using a combination of different accommodations to start with. You might, for example, spend some time in a guest house, then find a short holiday let, and possibly then a longer let whilst you weigh up your longer-term options. Some people may just never manage to buy their own property (and with prices in the Algarve pushing ever upwards, that may well be true of a large number of visitors now), and may look on renting as the only means of having their desired life out there.

HOTELS AND GUEST HOUSES

The range of commercial places to stay in Portugal rates from the ludicrously cheap, basic B&B (particularly away from the tourist areas), through a whole gamut of standard 1–5 star hotels and guest houses, right up to luxurious venues with price tags to match. Here is a general guide to accommodation in Portugal:

NAME	TYPE	BUDGET	FEATURES
Pousada/ Albergaria de Juventude	Youth Hostel	£	Clean, basic, some family rooms. Need youth hostel card.
Hospedaria/ Casa de Hóspede	Basic guest house	£-££	Modern, or in old buildings, not all en-suite. Breakfast not always provided.
Residencial/ Residência	Guest house	£-££	As above
Pensão	Guest house	£-££	As above
Hotel	Hotel	££-£££££	Standard to luxury
Albergaria	Inn	££-£££	As hotels, many with own bar/ dining areas.
Estalagem	Inn	££-£££	As above
Pousada	State-run luxury hotel	££££-£££££ depends on season	Mostly in traditional locations, e.g. former monasteries.
ALSO			
Quartos/ Dormidas	Room in private house	£-££	Basic, with use of family facilities. Meals by negotiation.
Parque de campismo	Campsite	£	Good network. Some with excellent facilities.
Solar	Country house	£££	Splendid rural living.
Turismo de Habitação	Room as guest in country house	££-£££	Stay and eat with family.
Turismo Rural/ Agro-Turismo	Farm stay/ Green Tourism	££-£££	Live and work on farms/eco-accommodation and lifestyle.

My husband and I recently did a three-week train journey in northern Portugal, in August (peak season), just booking into guest houses as we arrived at wherever we decided to stop off for a night or two. We had a couple of nights in fairly grotty accommodation in Oporto (near the station and as it turned out a veritable passing point for a number of ladies and their partners for the day!), and in another couple of last-ditch places as it was too hot to spend tramping around. These only cost us about £6 each a night so it didn't really bother us. The most we spent (as a treat), was for a magnificent room with an en-suite as big as you can imagine, in a beautifully restored 19th century town centre property, up in the far reaches of the Douro valley, with a breakfast to keep you going for a week, all at a price of £21 each!

Our average nightly spend over the journey, for what were, generally speaking, very clean, well-kept rooms in friendly surroundings, was about £12 each. So, if you are on a tight budget, you can still eke out a good stay for a reasonable outlay, provided you look around and avoid main tourist hotspots.

One thing to remember in town centres is, that many guest houses are situated on third and fourth floors above shops and other premises, therefore if you do not look for signs above you in the street, you may well miss some bargains. Don't be put off by grubby entrances – often when you get up to the establishment, it is actually quite decent. On the other hand, you may just have picked the local knocking shop! You can usually tell by the types of clientele sloping around at different times of the day. You can always walk back out, or just spend a single night there (which can often be an experience in itself!).

Many of the main guide books to Portugal list ranges of accommodation to suit all budgets; try the Rough Guide, Dorling Kindersley, AA Guides, Michelin, etc. You can also request lists of hotels from the Portuguese Tourist Information Office: Tel: 020-7494-5720, and email:

tourism@portugaloffice.org.uk.

Websites to check out:

www.ehstravel.co.uk
www.pousadas.pt
www.roteiro-campista.pt
www.pousadasjuventude.pt

Plus see Directory for more.

Most tourist information offices will book accommodation for you, and help you find something specific to your requirements. If it is high season, and they are busy, be prepared for a wait. See page 228 for a list of regional offices.

HOLIDAY LETS

Typical of the Algarve and other coastal resorts around Portugal, a holiday let can be anything from a couple of weeks, to a longer-stay of a few months over the winter period. Property is likely to be an apartment or holiday home, such as a villa or house on a complex, and the let is usually a straightforward holiday booking. The contract or agreement should be fairly self-explanatory and sets down the details for the rental period.

Property for this purpose is found through the same means as mentioned in the previous chapter: UK or Portugal-based English papers, overseas property magazines, estate agents, internet and word of mouth. David Littlewood, of north Lancashire, recommends the website run by Anne and Nick Parish, who have themselves recently moved to the Algarve: *Algarverentals@aol.com*. David and his wife regularly rent in the beautiful Algarve area around Silves.

Bill Fruish and family from Manchester found a house by word of mouth, available for a couple of months. They persuaded the owners to extend this to a longer let to enable them to find something more permanent. Bill sold his UK home in December 2003 and the whole family are now enjoying their new adventure in the Algarve.

Most travel agents can also book stays in villas for you, and carry brochures, or can order them, from specialist operators such as:

Simply Travel (Portugal and Madeira) – 020-8541-2222
Abreu Travel agency – 020-7229-9905
Portugalia Holidays – 020-8444-1857

So, what can you expect of a holiday let? Offered on a self-catering basis, most holiday property will consist of basic furniture and fittings: beds, wardrobes, bed-settee, table and chairs, kitchen appliances – often with just a cooker hob, and some cooking utensils. Generally bed linen is included, and with most short-term bookings, the price includes cleaning and domestic services, such as change of linen. For longer lets, it is worth checking if that is still the case, and how often it will take place. Over a period of a few months, you will find you may want or need to add to what is already provided in the place, to make it more practical or homely, for example tea towels, your own cleaning materials, items for the bathroom, candles, rugs or cushions. All can be bought very cheaply at one of the large supermarkets or hypermarkets, or at your local *feira*, or monthly market.

If you are using a holiday let as a longer-term accommodation solution, you may not necessarily want cleaning staff interrupting you as regularly as they might for a typical family on holiday. Come to an arrangement with the management services so that you are not disturbed every day.

Some years ago I went to Praia da Rocha on a long-term winter holiday deal which I found advertised in a UK high-street travel agent's (three months in a self-catering apartment). That was long enough (and certainly very cheap) to look around and find somewhere for a longer period. I ended up renting a flat in Silves from the lady who ran the Tourist Office there, simply because I went in and enquired about possible local lets.

LONG-STAY LETS

If you wish to consider renting as a longer-term option, there are likely to be three main routes to go down.

1. You rent from someone you have discovered by word of mouth, who are mainly going to be ex-patriots themselves.

2. You go through an estate agent and pay fees for their services above and beyond the price of the rental.

3. You try the private, Portuguese rental market.

By far the easiest route is to find property from another foreign resident who speaks English, so as to avoid any misunderstandings about responsibilities. Asking around in bars and places where ex-patriots tend to gather may come up trumps. Adverts in the English-speaking newspapers will give you further ideas. You could also place an ad yourself requesting property. Many foreigners are only too glad to find someone to let to if they are intending to spend time back in the UK. It may even be set up as a house-sit arrangement, where you look after someone's property for them in exchange for free accommodation. Some companies actually specialise in setting this up, but it is less complicated if you deal direct with the owners.

Many estate agents (Portuguese and foreign) will keep a number of rental properties on their books. The advantage of going via an agent is that they should sort everything out for you, from rental contracts to explaining your rights and requirements, to dealing with any on-going problems which may arise once you are in the property. They will collect the rent from you, and act as intermediary with the owners. Of course, for all this peace of mind, you will be paying on top of the rental price.

Looking in the private Portuguese rental sector is another possibility, and in some areas away from tourist estate agencies may be your only realistic means of finding somewhere to rent. Accommodation is advertised in daily regional and local papers, and often on signs on the property itself – *Aluga-se/Arrenda-se* (To let). 1–2 bed apartments in larger cities can cost €500–1000 a month, and much more in Lisbon and Oporto. You will need at least a working knowledge of Portuguese to understand what is on offer (some of the language in the previous chapter will help with adverts), and it may get difficult dealing with contracts and agreements if your language level is quite poor. If you have no other recourse, you could always ask for help at the local Tourism Office, English language school (if there is one), Town Hall (*Câmara Municipal*), or even high school, where there will be some teachers with a good level of English.

QUESTIONS TO ASK

However you find your rental property, there are certain questions you should ask before you sign up to any contract. You may also have your own specific points you wish to raise. Make a check-list and satisfy yourself on all points before moving in. This may include:

♦ What is the period of the contract/let?

♦ What notice is required on both sides? And should this be in writing?

♦ Is rent due monthly, weekly or up front?

♦ Do you need to pay a deposit? If so get receipts, find out the criteria for return of deposit and any conditions.

♦ Who pays the bills for amenities and any taxes and charges?

♦ What are the maintenance bills, e.g. for cleaning/garden/pools.

- What about damage? Check before you move in and mark anything already damaged on the inventory (list of what is in the place and what condition it's in).

- Who caries out repairs?

- Is decoration allowed?

- Who is responsible for problems with pipes and loos?

- Are pets allowed?

- What are the rules of access for the landlord, owner or agent, and notice of entry?

- What about insurance?

- How is the rubbish removed?

- How and where do you get replacement gas bottles?

Have meters read before you move in and keep a written check on them yourself. *Get everything in writing.*

RENT LAWS

It is common to have to pay a deposit plus up to two months' rent in advance. Budget for this as an initial outlay. The contract (*contrato de arrendamento*) is usually for a minimum of six months, and long-term for one year, renewable by mutual consent. It is common practice for the landlord to request a guarantor (*fiador*), who will pay the rent or damages if you default. If you are in any doubt, have a lawyer go through the contract with you before you sign up to anything. If it is in Portuguese, have it properly translated by a professional. Don't simply accept a translated copy from the owner or agent. I have heard of cases where the two versions have not clearly matched, leaving tenants in a precarious position *vis-à-vis* their rights.

SUMMARY

Renting is an extremely useful way of introducing yourself to life in Portugal before you take the plunge and invest valuable savings in real estate. If the option is open to you, consider renting short-term in a few different places, to try them out. If you are fairly decided on a location already, renting is a viable testing ground to see how things proceed. Whether you rent through an agency, or privately, from an English or Portuguese owner, make sure you understand what is on offer to you as tenant, what your responsibilities are, and exactly what you are signing up to. Get copies of everything in writing, and keep everything safely filed, including receipts for payments and bills. That way, you will have everything to hand if a query arises. Although renting may be seen as throwing money into the hands of owner or agent, for many people it can be the only realistic way of tasting life in Portugal, and at least if things don't turn out as you might have wished, you have fewer things to deal with should you decide to return to the UK.

Glossary of useful terms for renting

Aluga(m)-se	to let/rent
arrenda-se	to let/rent
aluguel/arrendamento	rent/lease
contrato	contract
depósito	deposit
contador	meter

fiança	guarantee
pagamento	payment
mensal/semanal	monthly/weekly
mobilado	furnished
sem mobília	unfurnished
equipado	equipped
garantia	guarantee/warranty
inquilino	tenant
inventário	inventory
lei de arrendamentos urbanos	property rental law
recibo	receipt
seguro	insurance
temporário	temporary/short-term

6

The People Involved

Along the way of purchasing your property, you will need the guidance and help of a variety of people, some more than others. The whole process can be overseen for you. Some foreign investors only ever have minimum contact with people in the chain – an initial meeting, some phone calls and picking up the keys – for others, it may be necessary to get more involved. Most people you will need to contact will have a good working knowledge of English – some will be excellent speakers of the language and very used to dealing with foreign buyers. In other cases, such as sorting out building instructions, it will pay to learn the rudiments of Portuguese (see also Chapter 11). Feedback from people who have been through the process is included in this chapter, but on the whole, the feeling is that, with good legal representation, the process itself can be painless and take less time than one might expect (see also next chapter).

ESTATE AGENTS

We mentioned in Chapter 4 the different means by which you can find out about property for sale. Estate agents can be UK-based, advertising in the UK press and specialist magazines, or have offices in Portugal with all the accompanying services one might expect of a normal estate agency (property details/photos/models of new complexes/access to further advice and professionals/letting services/property management). In Britain, a Code of Conduct established by the National Association of Estate Agents governs the behaviour of agents and gives certain protection to consumers, particularly in cases of misrepresentation of a property and its features. Unfortunately, no such law covers estate agents in Portugal.

In the Algarve the choice of (mostly) English-speaking agencies is bountiful. Many of them advertise in the English (or Dutch/German) publications there, and in specialist property magazines and supplements, such as *Algarve Property Advertiser*. You can pick these up in the resorts, at some tourist newsagents, Tourist Offices, and at the agencies themselves. For copies in the UK, ring the Distribution Company on 0179-225 229. Don't be afraid to visit a number of different agencies and pick up as much information as you can from each, before sitting down and sifting through it all.

Not all English-speaking agents will guarantee an efficient service, as Mr and Mrs X, in Lagos, found. They had found the ideal property, but the English estate agent lost interest in their offer. A year later, the house was still for sale, so they ended up buying direct from the owners.

After many happy years there, they are currently selling, and have encountered a number of ineffectual agents (both English and Portuguese), charging huge commissions to sell (4–5%). They have gone down the route many Portuguese people do, and have found that a notice on the wall of the house has brought in much more interest.

Mediador autorizado

Estate agents in Portugal, foreign or otherwise, should be officially recognised and belong to one of a number of Organisations, such as:

- Sociedade de Mediação Imobiliária
- Associação de Mediação Imobiliária
- Associação dos Mediadores do Algarve

Licensed agents have an official AMI number which should be displayed. Ask to see it if you are unsure. They will be known as a *mediador imobiliário* or *autorizado*. Despite this registration of agents, they are still not tied in with any form of consumer protection legislation. Interestingly, though, estate agent members of the Portuguese UK Chamber of Commerce have agreed to abide by the Code of the British Association of Estate Agents. For a list of members, contact the Chamber on Tel: 020-7494-1844. You can also contact the Federation of Overseas Developers Agents and Consultants (FOPDAC) for lists of their members. Tel: 020-8941-5588 or email: info@fopdac.com

Some estate agents are one-man, or family-run businesses, offering a bespoke, personal service. Others may be part of huge chains, conveyor-belt style sign-'em up and move-'em on. That is not to say that they are not professionals doing a good job, they may just be snappier, and more keen to get the process moving – which in fact may be just what you want. But don't feel pressurised in any way – remember this is an important point in your life, and involves life-changing decisions, especially in respect of parting with well-earned money. If you are not happy with an agent, there is no shortage, so try a different one.

Word of mouth is often a good starting point for many people: if you already know someone with property in Portugal, ask them which agent they used, or which they would avoid. Word soon gets round the foreign communities in the Algarve as to who is sound to deal with, and there are some now well-established agents out there. See Directory pages for a selection.

Elsewhere in Portugal, it is more likely you will be dealing exclusively with a Portuguese mediador. Again, as highlighted in Chapter 2, it is vital you have a modicum of the language to get you started in the process, plus access to an English-speaking lawyer. This may be arranged via the agent, who will have contacts locally. A number of Portuguese agents working in central and northern Portugal have now started advertising in the *Dalton's Weekly* newspaper, available in the UK. Anyone interested in property in central Portugal (*Coimbra environs*) may be encouraged to contact the agent recommended by Andrew B.: Eduardo Silva, of Villarq. Lda, in Penela, can be reached by email on: *villarq@mail.telepac.pt*, by phone: 23-9561 025 and on website: *www.villang.com*

SOLICITORS

Even if you are a fluent speaker of Portuguese, there is no point trying to go through this process under your own steam. Given the intricacies of what is involved, the Portuguese penchant for bureaucracy and its foibles, the absolute possibility for things to be misunderstood, all advice leads you to using a good, English-speaking solicitor (*advogado*) to oversee the whole process for you. If you are trying to complete your purchase whilst travelling backwards and forwards from the UK, you will need to give your solicitor Power of Attorney to move on your behalf. However, even if you are in Portugal during the time of the purchase, handing maximum power over to your solicitor simply gives you peace of mind, and minimises the risk of delay.

Having a good relationship with your solicitor will go a long way to aiding the smooth transition from purchaser to new owner, and there are many professionals working in Portugal who are very practised in this type of situation. So, how do you go about finding one?

◆ Word of mouth – the most important, if you have contacts who have been through the process, use them.

◆ Ask the advice of estate agents, but do not be led into using the same lawyer as is acting on behalf of the vendor.

◆ Ask the advice of AFPOP – they have lists of recommended professionals who are also members.

◆ Contact established companies, such as: Lita Gale Solicitors, Neville de Rougemont e Associados, (both with branches in the UK), and Bragança Bruno e Associados.

◆ Members of the UK Chamber of Commerce (see earlier contact details).

◆ Those regularly advertising in the local English news-papers.

NOTARY PUBLIC

The *Notário* is the official lawyer who is the only appointed person who can witness deeds of property transactions, so that new ownership can be registered at the land registry, and be fully binding on all persons party to the agreement (purchaser/vendor/financial institu-tions). You will use the Notary very rarely, and with the guidance of your solicitor. They also carry out checks on all the paperwork relating to the negotiation, preparing everything for official registration. They do not act as purveyors of guidance relating to issues surrounding the process. For advice on aspects such as finance, tax issues, inheritance etc, you need to talk to your solicitor and other professionals in the tax offices. The Notary may well not speak English, so you are advised to be accompanied by your lawyer when you attend for the signing and witnessing of paperwork. (Your lawyer will do this anyway if they have your Power of Attorney.)

SURVEYOR

Whilst it is not always necessary to have a full survey undertaken for your lender (if that is how you are financing the purchase) you may wish to have some kind of inspection done on the property for your own peace of mind, even if it is brand new. Even properties just 10 or 20 years old may now be prone to some serious defects, as many built during the past couple of decades were thrown up using inferior materials and methods.

You can, of course, carry out your own careful inspection, if you know what to look out for (look back to Chapter 3), and if you know anyone in the building trade, they are useful contacts to give you extra ideas, or even go with you if that is possible. Valuations and surveys can be done by estate agents, or they may be able to recommend someone to carry them out for you.

Builders are particularly useful on rural or older proper-ties where work may be needed. Getting quotes for work in writing is vital, especially if you want to use that as a bargaining tool in negotiating the price.

Portuguese surveyors can produce a report in Portuguese, which will need to be professionally translated, or at least explained to you by your solicitor. If you are in a part of Portugal where you have little access to English-speaking help, it is even more important to have clear insight into what the report contains. You may need to have it translated back in the UK, by an English native speaker (professional translators should always work *into* their own language). You may not find many with experience of Portuguese in the UK, but you can contact the National Centre for Languages (CILT), on 020-7379-5101 or for Professional Translating Services, check out the website: *www.blis.org.uk* If you have any difficulties, contact me via the publishers.

BANK MANAGER OR MORTGAGE LENDER

As there are different ways of raising finance to buy your property in Portugal, you may be dealing with:

◆ your own UK bank/ building society manager
◆ a local Portuguese bank manager
◆ a UK-based Portuguese bank official
◆ a financial adviser for off-shore companies.

In Chapter 10 we look in more detail at providing the funds for the purchase, so here we shall just briefly sum up the differences between the people you might be in touch with.

If you are raising money for a cash purchase, or tied to your own UK property, it is more than likely you will simply be in conversation with advisers at your own bank or building society. If you have built up a good rapport over the years with any individual at the bank, it is worth sounding them out first. Unfortunately, in this era of the flexible job market, it is rare to find that old fashioned manager who has been almost a family friend for 30-odd years. Still, today's banking personnel are well-trained and efficient, and should be able to refer you to the relevant bodies of advice if they themselves cannot help you.

Finding the equivalent service in Portugal can be hit and miss, although it must be said that the Portuguese banking system in general is much more efficient than you might realise, with hi-tec back-up and staff trained to high standards. Many speak English, especially in the Algarve, although it pays to be able to say at least a few pleasantries in Portuguese, if nothing else than to establish a friendly start. If you are looking in other parts of Portugal, you can rely less on English. Word of mouth, once more is an excellent starting point for recommendations for a bank, plus any advertised in publications by AFPOP.

Some of the main banks are:

◆ Banco Espírito Santo
◆ Totta and Açores
◆ Caixa Geral de Depósitos (savings bank)
◆ Atlântico (part of the Banco Comercial Português group)
◆ NovaRede
◆ Pinto e SottoMayor.

Barclays is one of a number of foreign banks in Portugal, although there are few recognisable English banks with offices there. Barclays has English-speaking staff, and produces its own information packs, including the summary *Buyer's Guide to Buying a Home in Portugal*. They have offices in Lisbon, Cascais and Porto. Their dedicated phone line in Portugal is: 21 791 12 22, and website: *www.barclays.pt* UK branches of Barclays can also get hold of the information for you. Their main UK international branch can be contacted on 020-7590-5768.

Some of the major Portuguese banks have branches in the UK (London), where you can speak to English-speaking staff well-placed to guide you on all financial aspects of buying property. They have a lot of experience of British people buying property in Portugal, and can offer the latest information on purchasing via a Portuguese bank.

Contact details for the major Portuguese banks with branches in the UK

Banco Comercial Português	020-7600-8380	*bcplondon@aol.com*
Banco Totta and Açores	020-7236-1515	*main@btax.co.uk* *www.bancototta.co.uk*
Caixa Geral de Depósitos	020-7623-4477	*paula.pegnall@cgd-uk.com* *www.cgd.pt*
Banco Espírito Santo	020-7332-4300	*www.bes.pt*

DEVELOPERS AND BUILDERS

Development is going on apace all over the Algarve, and to a lesser extent, in other parts of Portugal too. In some parts of the Algarve, you cannot help but trip over one billboard or another advertising the latest complex, holiday village, or apartment block. Most large-scale building projects are undertaken by big development companies, well-versed in mass-production of property, whereas smaller sites – perhaps just a few houses here and there – may be the domain of small companies (Portuguese or foreign-owned). In addition, smaller builders' businesses and one-man outfits may work on restoration and individual houses. There are many English, Dutch and Germans doing this kind of work in the Algarve, and offering all types of property maintenance services to, largely, ex-patriot communities.

Unless you are going to be buying off-plan, it is not usual to have consultation with a developer. Buying brand new, even when the building work is not entirely completed, is normally an area where you would be dealing with the estate agent or development sales team. Unless you have any real queries about the construction, you will probably never meet the developers themselves. However, it is worth looking around at other work carried out by the same developers, to get an idea of their quality. Ask at the Sales office on sites for details of other areas they have worked in.

Dealing with builders of smaller-scale jobs or with people you may wish to employ to help on your own house is an entirely different ball-game, and one covered in Chapter 9.

COMMUNITY OF OWNERS AND MANAGEMENT TEAM

If you are buying into a complex or holiday village, or into an apartment block with its own organisation, you will need to meet the people who run the residents' committee, or oversee the running of the site. The Community of Owners usually has its own elected administrators from amongst the property owners, and sometimes an outside person in addition. They function to make sure all owners in the urbanisation pay their due fees for communal services, such as pool and garden cleaning and maintenance, roads and buildings upkeep and repairs to communal areas. Rules and regulations governing the site and property are agreed and set in statute books, and owners must adhere to them. Owners are supposed to attend annual meetings, although in practice this is often not practical, and any voting can be done by postal proxy.

VENDORS AND LANDLORDS

It is possible, and there have been occasions, where people have negotiated directly with the vendors of a property, without any need for the intervention of agents. If the vendors are English-speaking, there is no real problem in discussing the property, the surroundings and negotiating a price. However, you will still need to enlist the help of a solicitor for all the official side of the process. I know of people who bought straight from vendors, and have remained firm friends with them since. However, it doesn't always work out like that, especially if there are any disputes over what has been agreed or what was included in the sale. That is why, however many times you are invited round for tea and cakes, you must come to a point where your solicitor takes over and gets things done in writing.

If you are renting property, there are pros and cons of meeting your landlord:

Pros	Cons
Good to put a face to the name and know who you are dealing with.	In some cases you really might not wish to know the background!
Establish friendly rapport from start – they can also be put at ease over the kind of people you are in the property.	Becoming too pally may make it more difficult to be firm with the business side of things.
Problems and queries can be discussed directly and with less delay.	Potential for upset may be better dealt with via a third party, i.e. an agent.
They may know the area better and be able to give you advice on how things work.	They may, of course, have bought the property for investment and have no idea about anything relating to it!

SUMMARY

It is not easy knowing where to start to find the right

people to help you in the process. You can help yourself by contacting professional organisations for lists of their members. Talk to as many people as possible about their own recommendations. Look for adverts in the English publications and send off for details of services offered by a variety of people. Don't jump at the first you find, take your time to compare services offered and fees suggested.

The Purchasing Process

Here is an overview of the purchasing process:

Find property or land and negotiate price
Carry out any inspections and surveys
Instruct a solicitor to act for you
Solicitor carries out land searches/negotiates contract of sale
Pay deposit and ensure payment lined up for rest of price
Sign Promissory Contract
Apply for Fiscal number/card
Open bank account
Solicitor obtains property registration certificates
Pay relevant property tax
Sign Transfer deeds
Register property at Land Registry and for local rates
Consider making a Will to cover property

And now, step-by-step:

GET PROPERTY OR LAND PLANS

Once you have found the property or land you are interested in, it is useful to have a copy of any plans relating to the site. These may be architect's detailed drawings, quite usual for new properties, and especially important if you are buying off-plan, or plans produced by the estate agents or builders/developers.

Having plans with measurements means you can calculate the real value of the property in relation to its dimensions and square metres, which may give you bargaining power over the price. Plans of the land (from the local Land Registry and Town Hall) may show up where main thoroughfares are located, water courses, boundaries, and other proposed developments. All these may have a bearing on the attractiveness of the site and the price at which it is being offered.

Off-plan purchases must be backed up by detailed plans, so that you know exactly what you are putting your money into. In many cases, you may have the option of modifying plans to suit your own design. Either way, make sure that when you finally agree on the design and dimensions, you have a copy of the final plans to refer to as building progresses.

CARRYING OUT INSPECTIONS AND SURVEYS

As mentioned in the previous chapter, it is difficult to find official Portuguese valuers and surveyors, but it is still important that the intended property is inspected, and if possible a report produced. This again may provide you with added power with regards to the price, but even more crucial, it should show up any potential defects or long-term problems which may eat away at your reserves of cash. In Chapter 3 we suggested a number of tell-tale signs to look out for when inspecting a property. Whether it is you, or someone under your instruction, make sure you check:

◆ Outlying area – ground, access, boundaries, rights of way.

◆ Walls (internal as well as external) – cracks, damp patches, missing render.

◆ Floors, especially if wooden, for signs of rot or worm – a high percentage of houses in Portugal suffer from termite infestation.

◆ Roofs – slipped/missing tiles, slumping, exposed beams, holes – flat roofs always subject to leaks.

◆ Plumbing – does it all work?

◆ Wiring – is it up to date? Are there certificates relating to when it was installed?

◆ Is electricity supplied by mains or generator?

◆ Water system – mains or tank?

◆ Swimming pool and filter system.

◆ Pipes, guttering, drains. Are they in good repair?

◆ Heating and air-conditioning systems. How old, what state and are they functioning?

Although it is not always possible in practice, especially if there is a risk that a property may be snapped up, it really is a good idea to see houses in both winter and summer conditions. What might appear attractive on a dry, sunny day in Spring, come wet November or February may well have turned into a dripping, soggy mess, surrounded by quagmires. Yes, it *does* rain in Portugal, increasingly so, but it also gets tinder-dry in the summer too – both extremes can have devastating effects on properties.

CONVEYANCING

This is the term for the work undertaken by your solicitor in respect of your purchase. It involves all the legal formalities, checking of documents, dealing with the vendor's lawyers, and overseeing the whole process. If you give your solicitor Power of Attorney (*Procuração*), all the stress of the Portuguese bureaucratic system can be alleviated, which is particularly comforting if you are trying to conduct the deal mostly from the UK.

As one resident said: 'most of the work is done by the lawyer so your own contact with Portuguese officials is minimal.'

One of the first things your solicitor will do is conduct searches at the local Land Registry to check the following details:

♦ That the owner is the person named on the registration document.

♦ The title deeds.

- That the property as described in the paperwork is the same as the one you are expecting to buy, i.e. size, outbuildings, land, etc.

- Whether the property has been previously subject to a mortgage – to ensure that this will be paid off with the proceeds of the sale.

- Whether there are any other charges against the property – e.g. unpaid loans, which will require payment from the proceeds – this is vital, as, under Portuguese law, debts stay with a property and not the individual person.

- Any interest in the property from third parties.

This last point is one of the most important. Because of the way Portuguese inheritance laws have always worked, it has been common for property to be divided up in wills, with members of the family being left various parts of the house. In order for the property to then be sold, all members have to be in agreement. This is fine when everyone is available for comment! There have been cases where family members who have gone off to far-flung parts of the universe, have returned in subsequent years laying claims to bits of property. Sometimes, though, even the most stringent of checks may not throw up these extraordinary cases – and it *is* with resale or older property that it happens. One couple I know, who bought some old property to renovate, were approached down the line by a chap from the village who wished to remove the roofing tiles from their barn, as that was his part of his inheritance. He did so, and promptly installed them on his own property down the hill!

It is also one of the reasons why so many older, rural properties in Portugal stand empty and unable to be sold; if family members cannot be contacted, it is unlikely a satisfactory sale can be reached, for fear of later comeback.

Your solicitor will also apply for the Habitation Certificate from the local Town Hall (*Câmara*). This proves that the building has been inspected by the local authorities and approved in respect of building regulations. Unless a property was built before 1951, the Deed of Transfer cannot be issued without this certificate. As there are various regulations governing different types and ages of property, this is work best done under good guidance. Your solicitor will also apply for the tax certificate relating to the property, which is held at the local Tax office. The Caderneta Predial contains information relating to the property, and its rateable value (see later).

PROMISSORY CONTRACT

Once all negotiations about the property or land have reached a satisfactory level to both parties, the process can move to the drafting of the contract. It is vital at this point that you are clear about all aspects of what you entering into, as if you back out once the contract is signed you will lose your deposit. If the vendor subsequently backs out, they will have to pay you double any monies you have already paid down. It is therefore abundantly clear that the closer contact you have with your legal aides at this point, the better for all concerned. Even if they have Power of Attorney for you, you must ensure you check the contract and are happy with what is laid out in it. There is very little comeback after it is signed. If you are in a part of Portugal where you have little access to English-speaking assistance, have the contract translated into English by a professional (English native translator) before you agree to sign.

PROVIDING THE FUNDS

You can pay for your purchase with cash, with a loan (possibly linked to a mortgage), or through an off-shore company. However, with recent changes to the property tax system in Portugal, the latter may no longer be an attractive option (see next section on Transfer Tax). Chapter 10 deals more with financial affairs, including different ways you can finance your purchase. At this point in the process you need to be able to pay your 10% deposit and have the funds available for the final payment on the property.

TRANSFER TAX

What used to be referred to as the Sisa tax (paid on transfer of properties between owners) has become subject to wide-ranging changes to the way property is taxed in Portugal. A new tax, known as *Imposto Municipal sobre Transmissões* (IMT), came into force in late 2003 as part of stringent measures to combat avoidance of taxes and underpayment through false declaration of property value. Under the new regulations, all properties will be subject to a valuation according to very strict criteria, and existing properties will be systematically revalued over a period of transition. The local tax department will play a stronger role in monitoring valuations, and if they suspect a property is being undervalued, they will be able to demand a revaluation, to reflect a price more in line with the realistic market price.

The new tax is being worked out according to a rather complicated formula, but in brief, will take into account:

◆ cost of building
◆ size
◆ type of use (residential, commercial, industrial etc)
◆ location
◆ quality of property and level of surrounding infrastructure
◆ age.

There will be a sliding scale of level of fees payable, ranging from 0–6%. Rustic property will have a flat rate of 5%, commercial property and land 6.5%, and *property bought through an offshore company 15%*. Given that particular rate, you may be persuaded to think twice about how you fund your purchase.

Your solicitor will be able to advise you further on likely tax level, and you can seek further help from the tax department (*Repartição das Finanças*). See also recommended reading in the Directory.

DEEDS – THE *ESCRITURA*
The *Escritura* is the official Deed of Transfer from the vendor to you, the new owner. It is a document which is signed either by you or your solicitor at the office of the Notary Public, and stays in the hands of the Notary for records. The Notary reads aloud all the particulars of the deed before everyone signs it. If you do not speak Portuguese you may wish to check with your lawyer that you understand exactly what is going on at each stage.

You can purchase as many legalised copies of the deed as you wish, but this is the only form of property 'deeds' which exist in Portugal. Once signed, the Escritura gives you official ownership, but you still have to register the property under your name with as little delay as possible.

REGISTERING THE PROPERTY

New ownership of the property or land must be carried out at the local Land Registry office (*Conservatória do Registo Predial*). You will need a legalised copy of the Escritura, the property tax certificate obtained by registering at the tax department, and you will complete a land registry form and pay a small fee. In due course, the new purchase details will be added to the property's title records.

RATES

You will also now be liable to pay rates on your property, previously known as *Contribuição Autárquica*, and under the new tax scheme as *Imposto Municipal sobre Imóveis* (IMI). As with the new IMT tax, properties will be subject to new valuations, and charges levied as follows:

New urban properties	0.2–0.5% new valuation price
Existing urban properties	0.4–0.8%
Rustic property	0.8%
Property held by offshore companies	5%

It is clear to see how the Portuguese government has taken a stance against the sort of dealings via off-shore companies previously favoured by many as a means of buying property in southern Europe.

For a comprehensive guide to the new tax regulations, read the latest booklet by Rosemary de Rougemont: *A Guide to The Portuguese Property Tax Reforms*, available from their UK offices, Tel: 01628-778566/Email: *ndr@nevillederougemont.com* or from the offices of the Portuguese UK Chamber of Commerce.

OTHER TAXES

You will also be liable for other taxes in Portugal, and it is vital you check your own personal situation carefully. Gift and Inheritance Tax has now been abolished, provided estates are left to surviving partners, children and parents. Beneficiaries who are neither spouse nor next of kin, will pay stamp duty of 10% on gifts and inheritances. If you have not already made a Will in respect of your Portuguese property, now is the time to seek advice.

If you are a resident in Portugal for tax purposes (i.e. resident there for over 183 days in any calendar year), you are subject to Portuguese Income Tax (*Imposto Sobre o Rendimento das Pessoas Singulares* – IRS) on your worldwide income. Non-residents are liable to tax on their Portuguese income. This applies to income derived from property (rental), and capital gains tax on the sale of any property. In order to purchase your property you will have had to apply for a Tax Card/Fiscal number. Income tax returns must be made by individuals, according to the regulations mentioned later in Chapter 12. Unless you are very clear about your tax position, it is not worth trying to guess what you should be paying.

SUMMARY

The process overall can be straightforward, if everything goes to plan, documents produced and signed on time, and provided that searches and contract negotiations do not throw up problematic issues. That is why it is so important to have legal representation, and not to go it alone. The whole process can take as little as a few weeks, or as long as a few months. One purchaser had agreed a price in January for his property, and both sets of lawyers instructed to complete in the June, as no one was in a rush. Even so, the process over-ran by a couple of weeks as certain paperwork was incorrect. They received the keys to the property just 2 days before they were due to fly back to the UK. Mr and Mrs G, from Lancashire, agree that the worst aspect is often being so far away (in the UK), whilst the process is going on in Portugal, but by giving Power of Attorney to a good lawyer, at least you know the deal can proceed in your absence.

GLOSSARY OF LEGAL PROCEDURES AND DOCUMENTS

Conservatória do Registo Predial	Land Registry Office
Título de Registo de Propriedade	Certificate of Title (Ownership)
Imposto de Selo	Stamp Duty
Câmara Municipal	Town Hall/Council
Licença de Construção	Construction Permit
Licença de habitação	Occupancy Licence
Caderneta Predial	Property registration certificate
Escritura	Deed of Transfer

Contrato de Promessa de compra e venda	Promissory Contract of Purchase of Sale
Cartão/Número de Contribuinte	Tax card/number
Imposto Municipal sobre Transmissões	IMT – transfer tax
Imposto Municipal sobre Imóveis	IMI – municipal tax/rates
Repartição das Finanças	Tax offices
Licença de utilização	licence of usage (commercial/industrial)

8

Buying a Timeshare or Property to Let

Not everybody wants, or can afford, outright ownership of a property, especially if it is just for holiday purposes. In this case, it has been common for the past few decades, and continues to be popular, to buy a share in a property, thus reducing initial outlay and still allowing frequent visits to be made. In other circumstances, property may be bought with the intention of renting it out whilst the owner is not there, or buying from the outset purely as a commercial, rental venture.

WHAT IS TIMESHARE?

The concept of **Timeshare** is not new; there are simply many more companies offering this type of shared ownership. In basic terms, what you are offered for a sum of money is a number of weeks annually in a property for the lifetime of the agreement. In practice, the scenario may be much more complicated, and there have been many cases highlighted where Timeshare scams have left investors bereft of their cash, and with nothing (or something very diluted) in exchange. On the other hand, there are very many thousands of contented Timesharers who happily visit their shared properties each year, and have had no complaints. In any case, it pays to weigh up this option very carefully.

It is no mystery how many of the Timeshare 'touts' try to get their business – many of you may have been accosted whilst out and about in the Algarve (as in southern Spain – their other big hunting ground). These so-called OPCs (Outside personal contacts, or Off-project contracts) hang around busy tourist areas, such as 'the Strip' in Albufeira, offering scratch cards to passers-by, with the lure of instant prizes. Once you have succumbed, in order to claim said prize, you are usually subjected to a trip to a presentation on the delights of owning your own time-share property. I have heard of people being bundled into cars and taxis and frog-marched into these talks, where they have sat for up to 6 hours listening to some spiel or other. In the searing heat of summer, it is not surprising that the weaker amongst us might be tempted to sign up to something simply in order to escape. And that is part of their plan of course! OPCs were banned from the streets back in the early 90s, but they have slowly crept back out. They are not allowed to work without a work permit, so try asking them for proof of their legal status.

The same kind of tactic may also work in the UK. You may receive a phone call informing of a win, or by post, and asked to attend an event where similar grinding down of resistance may lead to your falling into their hands. This pressurised selling methodology has come under a lot of scrutiny in recent years, and consumers are protected by a 'cooling off period' (usually 14 days), wherein you can change your mind and call the whole thing off without incurring any charges. However, not everyone remembers this, and those days can soon seep away and you may miss out on the opportunity to take a more measured decision about the situation.

If you find yourself in a situation like the ones mentioned, be firm but polite, and do not feel obliged to sign anything on the day. Even if you are cajoled by the presenters' constant reminders that the properties are selling fast and you will miss your chance, you must not put your name to anything you have not fully investigated and considered at home with all the necessary information in front of you. I know people who have sat through these events with raging headaches, feeling quite ill and trapped. I would say GET UP AND GO – whatever the reaction of the organisers.

But if Timeshare is something which attracts you, there *are* reputable companies you can go through, especially in many of the large tourist resorts in the Algarve (see next section). The Timeshare resort should be affiliated to one of two exchange organisations, which allow you to swap your weeks for time at other resorts around the world. The two groups concerned are RCI (Resorts Condominiums International) and II (Interval International). A fee is charged for membership of this scheme to allow you to exchange your holiday. As a Timeshare holder, you have a certain number of 'rights, in Portugal, such as the right to a certificate of ownership at the Land Registry, the right to sell, mortgage or rent out the purchased units, guarantees that the resort management will act in a way to ensure the property is well cared for. The Portuguese *Direcção Geral de Turismo* should approve such schemes in Portugal, which is one way you can check their validity.

OTHER PART-OWNERSHIP SCHEMES

Some resorts offer their own system of part-ownership, sometimes referred to as fractional ownership. It is basically the same concept, but may not offer exactly the same scheme as a normal Timeshare. It must still be approved by the Portuguese Tourist Board, but may offer a shorter time-span of ownership. According to Andy Burridge of the Vigia Group, who offer the *Parque da Floresta* resort in the Algarve:

'With fractional ownership, you buy a share of a company formed of your co-owners and your joint company owns the property. You have the full rights of ownership, including selling to others, renting, buying additional fractional shares or upgrading to outright ownership as your lifestyle and commitments change.'

Check out their website for further details: *www.parque-dafloresta.com*

Many resorts offer some kind of fractional ownership, alongside full purchase of properties. It is worth asking about all the options, and comparing a few, if that is the type of location which might suit you. Nowadays, though, it does not come cheap, especially in the up-market resorts built around golf and leisure courses. With the Vigia group, twelfth-shares start at around £25,000 and quarter-shares at about £78,000.

Whatever option you go for, have a lawyer check out the contract and regulations very carefully. Timeshare is not really an investment prospect, but when it works properly it can be a viable alternative to outright ownership, providing families with a guaranteed holiday home every year. On the other hand, as only part-owners, it makes the property less personal, and can really only be considered for what it is: long-term holiday accommodation.

THE PROPERTY RENTAL MARKET

Unless you have property in tourist areas, and let's face it, that really means the Algarve for the vast majority of people, you will find it pretty difficult to market a property for rent. Away from the southern coast you may be much more reliant on frequent advertising, using an agent (possibly Portuguese), and even Portuguese trade.

Be wary of companies at resorts offering buy-to-let schemes known as 'sale and leaseback'. What that usually means is that you buy the property, nominate a set number of weeks per year when you will inhabit it yourself, then lease it back to the company who lets it out for the rest of the year in return for a set income. Most experts believe that this is not the best way forward if investment is your goal, and say that if you can buy your property for cash in the first instance, or simply use the property you have bought for yourself for rental purposes part of the year, you will make more secure returns on it.

How to attract custom
You cannot just sit back and expect your property to attract custom without a bit of thought and preparation. Think about how and where you are going to advertise it:

◆ UK newspapers and specialist property magazines.

◆ Specialist magazines if there is a particular slant to the property or area, eg. ecology/bird-watching/artistic merit/walking holidays.

◆ English-speaking Press in Portugal.

◆ Internet – your own site or sign up to other specialist sites.

◆ Adverts and flyers around ex-patriot areas, bars and shops.

◆ Word of mouth – friends and family.

◆ Specialist villa holiday companies – brochures.

HOLIDAY RENTAL
The main holiday rental period is from April to October, during which time the right kind of property can make enough money to cover its finances for the entire year. Most financial experts agree that if you let your property for about eight months, including the peak summer family letting time in July/August, you can probably expect to make a return on your investment of between 5

and 8%, depending on size and location. A three-bedroom villa with pool can bring in £7–8,000 over the letting period, and a luxury villa on one of the prestigious golf resorts can render that kind of money in just a few weeks. But much depends on:

- location

- size of property – number of bedrooms

- quality and standard of finish

- pool

- accessibility to airport/highways

- proximity to amenities

- furnishings – for short-term rentals a certain amount of furniture and fittings must be included

- extra services, such as cleaning.

With holiday rentals, your turnaround of tenants or customers is likely to be fairly swift, as most people will be looking to rent for short holiday periods of 2–4 weeks. This means you need to be organised for the switch-over days, when the place is emptied, then needs to be cleaned and new bed linen and towels supplied before the next family arrives. You may have different types of clientele, depending on the time of the year, which may have a bearing on the furnishings and services offered: families will choose predominantly the summer months while spring and autumn may attract older couples.

LONG-TERM RENTAL

The prospects for longer-term rental are fewer. The main customers you may reach may include:

♦ People or families renting whilst looking for property or having a house built.

♦ Someone working on a set contract.

♦ People unable to afford to buy outright.

You will need to advertise predominantly in the English press in Portugal and the UK. If you set your rent at a reasonable level, you are more likely to gain interest for longer-term lets. Be prepared to be flexible and negotiate. After all, having the property let and being used is important for keeping it aired and having some form of income from it. Be clear from the outset, though, how long you are happy to let people continue staying there, and make sure everything is clearly set down in a contract.

LANDLORD'S COSTS

Once you have made your outlay for the property itself, you also need to take into consideration other, initial spends, and on-going financial implications. To start with you might have to pay for:

♦ Building work if applicable.

♦ Decoration.

♦ Furniture and fittings.

♦ Appliances – at least fridge/freezer, cooker, washing machine, and also possibly microwave, depending on the standard of service you wish to offer and price you can get from it.

- Bed linen and towels – multiple sets.

On-going costs may include:

- Advertising.

- Agent's fees (see later).

- Repairs.

- Replacement items damaged or removed!

- Management/community fees if the property is on a complex.

- Possible fees towards communal pool/gardens.

- Bills for utilities and local rates.

- Tax on business income.

If it is your intention to buy property with the primary function of a rental business, sit down first and budget for all possible spends, and weigh up whether this is really a viable business proposition. Remember, that with the holiday market, you are talking basically about 8 months of the year, with possibly some (cheaper) lets in winter months. Is that enough to cover your expenses? If not, how can you supplement it to cover any loans you may have had to buy the property? If you bought it outright for cash, your situation is more palatable, but even so, if you want to use this as a means of income, it has to stand on its own feet for you.

LANDLORD'S RESPONSIBILITIES

As landlord, you cannot overlook the fact that you have certain responsibilities to your tenants, to your home, and to your neighbours and surroundings.

Your property	Your tenants	Your neighbours/area
Maintenance	Well-presented property	Keep property in good repair/well-presented
Decoration	Fair rent	Ensure tenants are not nuisance
Replacement of furniture and fittings when old or damaged or stolen	Fair and clear contract	Payments to community/ management
Maintain payments for taxes and utilities	Swift dealing with problems	Make yourself known
Insurance	Be easily contactable	Informing when property to be empty
Security	Safety requirements	Ensure rubbish disposed of

USING AN AGENT

Many people decide that they would prefer an agent to handle their rental property for them. Often this is because they are not there themselves the whole year to keep an eye on the property and see tenants in and out. Or, for others, it is simply more convenient having experienced professionals take care of the business for them, especially if they are either busy themselves, or are not entirely comfortable dealing with the public, especially where problems arise. If you are not going to be in Portugal all year round, using an agent is probably your only option. Some people are lucky and find neighbours or friends who will oversee the rentals for them, even hiring locals to carry out cleaning, gardening and any handiwork necessary. But if you don't know anyone who can do that for you, you will need to employ an agent.

Agents are not difficult to find – in fact most real estate agencies also offer the service of property management, or some specialist firms also operate, mostly in the Algarve. If you buy in a resort or complex, the management will also offer the service – for a fee. It is worth asking around a few agencies first to compare their fees. Usually they will expect to receive up to 15% of your rent, and for this will offer varying levels of service. Check first and make sure you have a clear list in writing of what they will actually do for you, e.g.:

- Sorting out contracts/rental agreements.

- Letting people into the property.

- Arranging cleaning.

- Collection of rent and payment to you (via bank).

- Carrying out minor repairs when necessary.

- Advertising.

A recommended English-run rentals agency in the Algarve is *Actividades Turísticas de Burgau* (ATB), in the western Algarve, run by Sam Filisberto and her Portuguese husband Nuno. She says:

> 'Larger villas with pools and new properties are in constant demand. Lots of places are being converted and refurbished at the moment so facilities can be upgraded to keep up with tourist requirements.'

BUSINESS AND TAX IMPLICATIONS

If you let your property out in return for any payment, you are liable to pay tax on that income. Whether you are registered for tax in Portugal (as a resident), or in the UK, you must declare your income on your tax return. You can claim certain deductions against the income. See Chapter 12 for more on your tax situation, or contact your local tax department for guidance. The tax rules in Portugal, as elsewhere, can be complex and in order to avoid not paying correctly, or missing out on legitimate allowable expenses, it is best to seek further advice from the local *Finanças* department, or a financial adviser in Portugal.

AFPOP have a series of very useful information sheets covering all aspects of housing, and have a list of professionals recommended by them.

SUMMARY

Buying a share in a property is a means to enjoying time in Portugal for many years without the total capital expense of purchasing a whole house. If you find a reputable timeshare company you will have few difficulties. Renting out your property, either in the short or long-term, is fairly easy to do in tourist areas provided you do your homework first and consider your budget and the practicalities of looking after the property and the business.

Have you:

♦ fully investigated a number of Timeshare companies?

♦ obtained sufficient information to make a sensible

decision on a part-ownership scheme?

- made a budget for possible expenses for your rental property?

- taken into account on-going payments?

- shopped around for services and prices from agents?

- considered your tax situation?

- contacted AFPOP and other useful organisations?

9

Renovating or Building Your Own House

Not everyone wants a brand new house or apartment. Some people choose to find something more typically Portuguese, with more character, which may need a certain amount of renovation or decoration. Others may decide to find a plot of land in a location of their choice, and have a house built to their own specification, even doing a lot of the work themselves. Anything is possible, and in the Algarve you will find no shortage of trades-people to help you (many foreign). Even in other parts of Portugal you should find enough local help to sort you out, although you may have to be more flexible with your deadlines!

FINDING THE PLACE YOU WANT

If you are looking for a piece of land, or older property, it is probable that you will be searching in a totally different area to the densely-populated tourist complexes of the central Algarve. Although it seems at times like the whole of the southern coast is just a seething mass of modern villas and apartment blocks, only a couple of miles or so away from the beaches gets you into more rural areas. This means that you can still benefit in many cases from local amenities and infrastructure, whilst being located slightly away from the melée. Further afield still, and the choice is even wider, although bear in mind what we said in the previous chapter about inheritance problems sometimes virtually rendering an older house unsaleable.

Estate agents do have plots of land and some older houses for sale, so they are often one port of call. Use all the means mentioned in Chapter 4 to look for places, but expect to drive around a bit more. The Portuguese often just paint signs on the side of their property, with a phone number whilst foreigners are more likely to put ads in the local ex-patriot papers.

Be open-minded about what is on offer, and its potential. Try to be visionary in your approach! What at first glance appears to be a ramshackle shed, may actually be a wonderful rustic house in the making. On the other hand, be realistic too. Older houses as projects can eat into your finances, and are often more expensive to heat. You may be able to compromise, you may be happy to live in more humble surroundings, you may have enough cash and time to undertake a superb renovation job; be shrewd in your judgements and be clear about what you (a) would love and (b) could live with.

Mr and Mrs W, from Huddersfield, advise caution:

> 'Look for a house that is already built – we've heard
> that renovating a broken-down cottage can be very
> expensive (or building from new) and take a long
> time.'

But with caution in hand, how can you proceed without
too much pain?

RENOVATING

The recent frenzy of DIY programmes on our TVs has
given all but a very few the penchant for going in, ripping
out, and launching into re-model and modernise mode.
Sales at DIY stores are at their highest ever, and as a
nation, we have become obsessed with making our own
homes more beautiful. Now there's nothing wrong with
making improvements, but, as someone with a father in
the building trade, I have to admit that it seems almost
carnivorous to go into a property and start pulling walls
down and ripping out existing features. Not to say short-
sighted and in some cases downright dicey.

If you are buying a property to renovate, think about the
current space it offers and how that space is divided up.
Are the rooms and their layout practical for your own
purposes? If it is old property, the rooms are likely to be
much smaller than their modern equivalent, but they may
have their own character to compensate. If you are
considering knocking through rooms, you must be sure
the remaining walls are supporting ones and can take the
strain of the rest of the building. You will almost

inevitably need to insert supports. This is work best left to professional building firms.

What else may you need to look at in terms of renovation?

- The roof – is it sound? Does it need new tiles or replacements

- The roof joists, especially if there is any suspicion the old ones are rotten or infested.

- Window frames – try to replace like with like, i.e. don't spoil an old house by putting in plastic windows, they never retain their original character. Unfortunately, the climate in southern Europe leads to much more damage to wood features, so many people do choose to replace with PVC or aluminium.

- New wiring and plumbing systems?

- Heating – the house may not have had any form of heating before. Now you can consider central heating, underfloor, solar-powered, natural fuel-burning fires or stoves.

- Adequate insulation and draught prevention?

- Water system – depends very much on local availability of mains, but you may be able to modernise what already exists.

- Floors – replace rotten boards.

- Interior work such as plastering ready for decorating.

If the work you are intending to carry out is fairly minimal, and will not alter the structure or external appearance of the property, it is not usual to require planning permission, or a building licence. However, for more substantial works, you will have to present certain documentation to the Council (*Câmara Municipal*) and seek their approval for the project. In any case, it is best to check with them whatever your plans might be, rather than get part-way through the work and find you do not have permission.

PLANNING APPROVAL
In order to seek approval, you will need to show:

- certificate of responsibility from the architect in charge of the project
- description and detailed plans
- estimate of cost
- work schedule
- excavation plans
- structural information
- designs for installation/renewal of electrics, gas, phones, water and drainage
- plans for thermal insulation and, if necessary, sound-proofing
- plans for ventilation.

The local authorities will then consult on the project, and if you have approval you are granted the licence, or *alvará de licença de construção*. Before building work can commence, the builders have to show their own licence and insurance details to the Council, and after all the works have been carried out, the Council must inspect the property to see if everything has been done in accordance with the original licence. If all is in order, they will issue you with the licence for use (commercial) or occupation (*licença de utilização/habitação*). You may need to update the entry in the Land Registry if substantial differences now exist. Many properties improved in this way are also eligible for some tax relief from the property rates, even under the newly-imposed regime. Check at the local Tax Office for details.

If you will need to stay in the property whilst you get on with the work, make sure at least a couple of rooms are habitable, and that you have access to cooking facilities and somewhere to go to the loo. Without these basics, you will find the stress of living in a dusty, upside-down building site will really get to you and spoil what otherwise might be an exciting venture.

BUILDING YOUR OWN

If you are not in a rush to get moved into your new home, one final option worth considering is to buy a plot of land and have a house built to your own design. There are advantages to this. You have the choice of location, control over the size and design of the house, can check the quality of workmanship, can install modern systems right from scratch, and have the satisfaction of doing your own thing. There are downsides too: it may take you longer to find the ideal plot of land, you will need planning permission and may not be able to do everything you want, if you are not constantly on site you will *not* be able to check the standard of work, it may (will!) run overtime and budget.

Even if you are fairly accomplished building workers yourselves, you will still need to enlist the help of professionals such as:

◆ surveyor or qualified builder to check the land and area
◆ architect or engineer
◆ builder/ contractor
◆ tradespeople
◆ lawyer to check contracts and licences.

Before you can go ahead you will have to have plans approved by the Council. You may have a rough idea of what you want the finished house to be like, but you need to sit down with an experienced architect and have proper plans drawn up to submit for approval. It is important that you ultimately agree with what the plans depict, so don't be afraid of getting various designs drafted before you settle on one. Your architect should be affiliated to a Professional Association, and a builder should have his own licence (*alvará*) and insurance for his employees.

DEALING WITH BUILDERS

In the Algarve, many building firms and tradesmen are foreign (mostly English, Dutch or German). There are also local Portuguese companies. Large construction firms often employ African and, increasingly, Eastern European, labourers. Although your first choice may be to find an English builder, without recommendations, there is still no guarantee of the quality of work, or the honesty of the person in question. Cowboys exist in the Algarve as much as in the UK – and sometimes get away with rogue practices more easily as they can pack up and disappear in the blink of eye. One resident told me that many English contractors fall by the wayside because they expect English rates per hour. To find a reputable builder or craftsman, as with many situations we have mentioned thus far, word of mouth is the best starting point. Beyond this, ask for lists of members of AFPOP in the trade, or their recommendations, plus read their useful information sheets on construction and renovation.

Portuguese builders are usually good at their work, hard-working once they get going, and normally honest. The main problem, according to anyone who has ever employed any, is that they are totally unreliable in terms of timing! They may turn up every so often, work for a while, down tools and go for long lunches, come back a few days later, and always with a friendly '*até amanhã*' (see you tomorrow). It is almost impossible to tie them down, and you may cause friction by trying too hard. In advance of this, build extra time into your master scheme, and have contingency plans for when work comes to a standstill. It is made even more difficult if you are not to hand to crack the whip. Mr M. in Lagos, says:

'We have had two major pieces of building work done, both by Portuguese builders, and we have been mainly satisfied, despite a few details being not quite right.'

Builders and contractors you may need to contact include:

- *construtor*   builder
- *arquitecto*   architect
- *pintor*   painter

- *pedreiro*   bricklayer
- *carpinteiro*   carpenter
- *canalizador*   plumber
- *decorador*   decorator
- *electricista*   electrician
- *engenheiro*   engineer
- *contramestre*   foreman
- *trabalhador*   labourer

Case Study – Barbara's building (true story)

Planning permission took two years to obtain. Building plans were passed by the Câmara after about six months, then when the engineering plans went in, they all had to be passed by the same architect. He then died so we had to start the process again. The second time whilst waiting for approval there was an election and a change of council. Because the plans had been passed we started building without approval about eighteen months into the procedure. The building work took about 12 months for the shells of two houses. A work book (diary) was completed by the builders and signed at each stage by the architect. This was then passed to the Council in order to gain the habitation licence.

The worst aspect of the process was the waiting and the frustration of not speaking the language. A lot of time and effort was lost when things were misinterpreted on both sides. Then there was the bureaucracy. For example when having electricity put in we were not allowed mirrors in the bathroom because they were not earthed. There was no plug socket in the kitchen that could be reached when standing at the sink. Although they did put a socket next to the bathroom sink which we didn't ask for! When the electrics were finally in and an inspector came from Lisbon to pass it we were told we could put the mirrors back up in the bathrooms!

Barbara's advice:

Start a diary of events from Day 1. Be prepared for things to take longer and cost more than quoted. Be prepared for things to go wrong. Try to keep a sense of humour and try to think of building in Portugal as old-tyme dancing – one step forward, one to the side and two back!

When using builders, whether Portuguese or foreign, make sure you have a quotation in writing for the cost of the work. Estimates are fine when you are making initial enquiries, but are often too woolly to work with as an on-going measure. In any case, costs have to be presented in your plans to the Council. If additional work arises as the project is underway, check it is absolutely necessary, and tie them down to costs. Usually you will pay by instalments, in accordance with the stages of the work, with a down payment to start with to cover the initial costs of materials. All aspects of the fees and stages should be in writing. If work is not completed by certain dates, you may have more leeway for negotiation on price. Be firm! The contract should also make reference to the length of guarantee for the work. It is normal practice for a builder to have to correct any faults within one year, but there should also be a longer guarantee for hidden faults. Make sure you, or your architect, also check the quality of materials being used. It is ideal if someone can visit the site at regular intervals (once a week if possible) to keep an eye on things.

LOCAL AND REGIONAL PLANS

When planning your dream building project, it is vital you take into account at the initial stages any local or regional plans in place, or in the pipeline. Before you step in and make your purchase check for:

◆ Local urban development plans which curb building, such as the PROTAL law in the Algarve, in existence for a number of years, and limiting what can be done in rural areas.

◆ Environmental issues/plans – there is particular concern to protect land near waterways and near agricultural land.

◆ Planned new highways.

◆ Use of land, e.g. for commercial purposes – could affect whether you can run a business.

◆ Any possible future plans for the use of the land which may affect the type of construction.

The place to look for plans is the Town Hall (*Câmara Municipal*). Each Municipality now has its own Development Plan, which outlines proposed plans for future development, and where existing areas offer better opportunities for construction. Certain plans may affect the price of the land or property – up or down, so it is in your best interest to study them carefully. You may just make the right decision to walk away and rethink your strategy.

THE PURCHASE PROCESS

If you decide to go ahead and buy an older property or plot of land, the purchase process is the same as outlined in Chapter 7. What you need in addition is all the paperwork relating to the planning permission and work schedules. It is just as important with a piece of land that your lawyer carries out detailed land searches to check there is no outstanding debt allocated to it. Mortgages, loans and third-party charges on the plot may all impede the sale of it unless there is some guarantee that all monies will be paid before the sale goes through.

A useful summary of things to consider is provided by the Consular Section of the British Embassy in Lisbon, in their guidelines entitled: *Possible pitfalls in the purchase of residential property in Portugal and review of planning considerations relating to the purchase of land for building residential property.*

Further, general advice on building and renovation is available on the useful website: www.newskys.co.uk – there are various articles about properties, life abroad, and practical advice.

GETTING A GRANT

In recent years the Portuguese government has concerned itself with the promotion of what it perceives to be 'quality tourism', especially in rural areas. Some people of late have called that to account in the face of large-scale tourist villages which have been allowed to go ahead in conservation areas. However, some grants are available for people who wish to buy property and run it for tourist purposes, such as Bed and Breakfast or eco-holidays. Help may be offered towards the cost of the property itself, provided you remain in it for a set number of years. For detailed information about business grants and incentives, contact ICEP (Portuguese Travel and Tourism Office) London telephone 020-7494-5720 or email: *tourism@portugaloffice.org.uk*

PROS AND CONS

When considering whether to renovate or have your own house built, it is worth weighing up the advantages against those of buying brand new or modern resale properties.

Pros	Cons
Older property has more character.	Subject to local/regional plans.
Stamp your mark on by renovating.	Expense of building.
Choice of more rural location.	Older properties can be more expensive to run.
Satisfaction of doing what you want.	Can take time to finalise.
More authentic approach to life in Portugal.	Utilities may be more difficult to maintain.

SUMMARY

Renovating an older property, or building from scratch are both very real options in Portugal. Although the majority of people buying there opt for new properties, those who have decided on this alternative have generally managed well. If you take on board the right professional help and advice, make sure you follow planning guidelines properly, have someone on site to oversee proceedings, and try to not get frustrated by how long things might be taking, then you'll get through. Budget for more than you expect, build in extra time, be patient and try to see the funny side of things. Keep an account of what's going on; if nothing else, one day you might end up writing a bestseller based on your trials and tribulations in the sun!

⑩

Money Matters

Having the dream of a place in the sun is one thing; being able to afford it and all the associated costs linked to it is quite another. Before you head off into the sunset with your dreams of days languishing by the pool, or indeed even plans for an established home or business, take a step back, sit down and work out if your finances will stretch that far and beyond. In the light of the newly-implemented property tax reforms (1 January 2004) in Portugal, it is also vital that you weigh up very carefully your options for paying for the property in question, and seek professional advice on your own situation before you get too far down the line.

PROPERTY PRICES

It is abundantly clear to anyone who has visited the Algarve in recent years that property development has gone on apace, with many more golf and leisure-type complexes, and apartment resorts than could have been envisaged just a few years ago. Despite the PROTAL legislation of the early 90s, which aimed to curb widespread construction and thus avoid the scenario of the neighbouring Spanish Costas, developers have found areas they have been able to get their digger-teeth into, and, behold, an ever-expanding array of villas! Now, of course, supply can only mirror demand, and the popularity of southern Portugal as a holiday and retirement destination has grown enormously over the past decade, leading to an increase in the number of houses required. The vast majority of these are brand new apartments and villas. Demand has now outstripped supply in many parts of the Algarve, and with the standard of facilities and services offered on some of the luxury complexes now much higher, prices reflect quite staggering levels of increase.

To give you some ideas of prices for new property, based on property guides January 2004:

Location and type	Minimal price
3-bed apartment in Lagos area	£105,000
Apartment overlooking marina at Vilamoura	£175,000
2-bed apartment in retirement village, Faro surrounding area	£120,000
Town house Parque da Floresta golf resort	£190,000
5-bed villa Monchique	euro 450,000
4-bed villa near Lagos with pool, garage, wine cellar	euro 750,000
4-bed villa with pool and large plot near Loulé	euro 850,000
1–2 bed apartment on condominium near Lagos	£160,000
1–2 bed apartments in condominium in Albufeira	euro 130,000

And, new property elsewhere in Portugal:

Campo Real Golf development outside Lisbon offers apartments and townhouses starting at about £200,000. For your money you also have access to the golf course, health club and spa, tennis club, golf academy and equestrian centre. Around the Sintra area, the Belas Clube de Campo is another luxury estate offering similar properties ranging from apartments from £120,000 to villas from £350,000 up to a million pounds. Similar developments can be found near Óbidos, Cascais and Estoril, the latter two being traditionally popular resorts along from Lisbon.

If you are not bothered about having your life on a developed resort complex, or closed, security-conscious condominium, you will find new flats and houses in any part of Portugal, advertised in the Portuguese press and agencies, with prices reflecting the local market.

Re-sale and older properties come in a lot cheaper, but in the Algarve, and certainly going through estate agents, prices may still seem steeper than you imagine. A 2 or 3 bedroom flat in the Algarve may cost from around 70,000 euros. Rural, typical farmhouses and rustic buildings which have been renovated will be upwards of 150,000 euros. Those needing work may be found from 100,000 euros. You can find beautifully-restored houses around the Lisbon area – but still at a high price. For example a recently-restored Portuguese family house in Estoril, with 3 bedrooms and a collection of other interesting rooms, but still needing some restoration was being offered at the time of writing for 700,000 euros. Once out into the real Portuguese countryside, though, and away from any tourist areas, the prices start to become much more attractive. A couple I know who regularly buy, renovate, and sell rustic properties in central Portugal recently had a 2-bedroom house with wine cellar for sale at about £48,000. Look around and you will be able to find properties from about £25,000. It is certainly not as cheap as buying in France, where you can still buy fairly large rustic houses in reasonable condition for quite a pittance. However, if you are prepared to put in the work of visiting less crowded places, you will be rewarded with relatively cheap houses.

The current tax reforms which have just been imposed are hitting a lot of home-owners who bought through off-shore companies and who will not be able to afford to maintain the new tax payments, nor pay to have the property transferred to an 'on-shore' mortgage. In the light of this tricky situation, many owners have been selling up, and a higher number of properties than normal have been coming up for sale, the knock-on effect of which is to give buyers more purchasing power, and bring prices down.

Statistics on houses valuations, from the Portuguese National Institute for Statistics, found prices rising all over Portugal in 2002, and on average by 1.6% on the previous year. Whilst property in the Greater Lisbon area averaged 1,421 euros per square metre, up in wild Trás-os-Montes it was only 759 euros. The greatest rise in prices was seen in the Alentejo and the Algarve.

ARRANGING PAYMENT

There are different ways you can finance your purchase. Whether you are buying brand new, off-plan, re-sale or a plot of land, it doesn't matter – the choice is really yours, depending on your own financial circumstances. However, consider the options very carefully, and with professional advice, especially in the light of the new taxation regulations, which have a direct impact on purchase.

PAYING WITH CASH

A large number of people are lucky enough to have been able to raise the cash in the UK to buy their property outright. Those who bought a few years ago were able to do so when prices were still relatively low in Portugal. Nowadays, that option may be increasingly difficult for all but a small number of people. If you are in a position to sell your UK home at the inflated prices of the moment, making a fat profit in the process, that is one obvious way to release the cash to buy outright. But that period will not last forever, and as the UK market slows down, the margin for net profit on house sales will decrease accordingly. However, cash purchases do remain the easiest option if you can manage it. All you need to do is ensure the cash is available in your own bank account, and when the property purchase goes through, the correct amount is then transferred by bank credit transfer to the relevant bank in Portugal. This side of things will be overseen by your lawyer, so all you need to do is make sure the cash is there in the first place.

REMORTGAGING UK PROPERTY

If you have UK property which has risen in price over the last few years and you are sitting on a handsome sum of equity in it, you may wish to opt to release a lump sum by extending the length of your original mortgage, or starting with a new one. This may be an option if you wish to keep hold of your UK property. You may well have sufficient to buy your Portuguese property outright, whilst still holding on to your UK home. However, it is usual in these circumstances that your Portuguese property will be secured against the UK one, so that your bank will have a 'charge' on the property. If you subsequently run into difficulties in repaying the extended, and possibly higher, mortgage payments, there is always the risk that the bank can ultimately 'call in' that charge and you could lose your home.

It is worth shopping around these days to find beneficial rates, even for remortgaging. You may be able to find a preferential rate elsewhere, with a lender who will re-value your property, and set up a mortgage according to a new loan period. If you find out some quotes first, you can also use them as a bargaining tool with your own lender. Often they are willing to re-negotiate terms and fees if they think you are about to take your custom elsewhere. The only caveat here is that, should interest rates in the UK suddenly take a hike, you will be left with a much higher level of payment against your UK home, and may therefore find it difficult to maintain the loan on the property.

Remember to build into your budget any arrangement fees your lender may impose for remortgaging services. That may typically be around £300.

TAKING OUT A PORTUGAL-BASED MORTGAGE

A local mortgage has different requirements and possibilities, although the process of setting up a mortgage is pretty much as it is in the UK, where the bank or lender sets up a loan on the property in question, and retains a legal charge on it in case of default of payments. Applications will be considered based on the valuation of the property, the financial situation of the applicant, and the applicant's credit history and age. A loan is usually for a maximum of 15 years only, and will not normally extend beyond the retirement age of 65. Usually only up to 75% of the value of the property will be loaned, thus leaving you to find the balance yourself in cash. If you intend to let your property other than to friends and family, it is advisable to check first with the lender whether they allow 'commercial' use of the property, as it may alter the rate of interest you are charged.

It is usually quite tricky negotiating direct with a Portuguese bank yourself, unless you have already had an account out there and know you can talk things through with your local manager. People who want a Portuguese lender are better advised to go through a British broker who knows the system a little better. However, some UK lenders, including Abbey National, Halifax, Conti Financial Services and HSBC, also offer mortgages in Portugal.

Abbey National: 0800-449090/*www.anoffshore.com*
Conti Financial Services: 01273-772811
Propertyfinance4less (European mortgage UK broker): 020-7924-7314/*www.propertyfinance4less.com*

There are also Portuguese banks with offices in London who can arrange mortgages too, such as Banco Totta e. Açores, Tel: 020-7236 1515/ Email: *mortgage@btax.co.uk* See also Directory.

It is better overall to have a mortgage in euros. With Portugal in the eurozone, having both your property value and loan linked to it in the same currency, makes it less likely to fall victim to any fluctuation in the strength of the euro against sterling.

Barclays International bank in Portugal offer a mortgage for non-residents. It is based on a 15-year loan, up to 70% of the value of the home. You can contact their Portuguese main office direct on: 351-21-791 12 22, by email: *banco.telefonico.pt@barclays.co.uk* and on a website: *www.barclays.pt* In the UK ring: 0207-977-4357

To find a specialist broker dealing in local mortgages, contact the Federation of Overseas Property Developers, Agents and Consultants for a list of regulated operators. Tel: 020-8941-5588

For more information on overseas mortgages you can check out the website: *www.mortgageoverseas.com*

For further information on Portuguese banks and their schemes, try the website of the *Financial Times*: *ft.com*

USING AN OFF-SHORE COMPANY
It is estimated that, over the years, almost 75% of people buying in Portugal have done so by the popular method

of using an off-shore company. This has been a *modus operandi* in the property investment world for a good number of years, and up until recently has worked well. A financial company would set you up with an off-shore company (often based in places like Gibraltar or Jersey), under whose name you would buy your property. One of the main advantages was that you could avoid hefty inheritance (capital gains) taxes on succession. Now the authorities in Portugal have started a huge clamp-down on this type of investment, in an attempt to swoop on large numbers of people who have managed to avoid paying appropriate taxes – the system has often been open to abuse. Under sweeping reforms introduced on 1 January 2004, called the *Reforma do Património*, stringent regulations came into force regarding property taxes which will have a dynamic effect on owners' contributions.

We outlined the new tax scheme in Chapter 7, and pointed out how existing property will be revalued, and new levels of tax will be imposed annually. For anyone with an off-shore company, that level of tax will now be an annual 5% of valuation for council rates.

In relation to how this will affect anyone wishing to go down this route from now on, the property purchase tax (also described in Chapter 7) will be a payment of 15% of purchase price, which on a villa of a value of £250,000 (commonplace now in the Algarve), represents an extra £37,500 in purchase tax, and annual £12,500 rates. Portugal has produced a list of what it considers 'black-listed' countries, from where it will not accept any off-shore companies. The only remaining acceptable ones are Malta, Delaware (USA) and New Zealand. However, even these countries may find themselves excluded eventually. All advice emanating from financial organisations now is simply **do not consider an off-shore company as a viable means of financing your purchase**.

The most up-to-date guidance on all the new tax reforms is the, already mentioned, booklet by Rosemary de Rougemont: *A Guide to the Portuguese Property Tax Reforms*. Good advice is also available from people listed in the Directory.

BUDGETING FOR CAPITAL COSTS

At the time of purchasing the property you will need to budget for the initial deposit of around 10% of purchase price, plus the following costs, mainly for legal services and officialdom and based on the purchase price/ valuation of the property (all are approximate as they depend on type of property and situation):

♦ lawyer's fees for conveyancing – 1–2 %
♦ fees to the Notary around 400 euros
♦ Land Registry fees + / − 1%
♦ property transfer tax up to 8% valuation of house, 15% for off-shore purchases.

It may well be that, if you are buying brand new or off-plan property, many of the above costs are wound up in the price of the overall package you are buying into. Make sure you know what is included in the sale price, and what will be paid for by you under separate negotiation. Ask your lawyer to itemise everything you are likely to pay.

Don't forget, too, that you may need to allow a budget for renovation work, or re-decorating. If you are doing that kind of work yourself, there are now a number of large, DIY superstores in the Algarve, where you can get price leaflets to work out estimated costs of materials.

BUDGETING FOR ADDITIONAL COSTS

Whilst some homes may come ready-furnished (often resale properties have some items of furniture, and part-ownership schemes come with a ready-furnished package), you may also need to budget for items such as:

- your own furniture and fittings
- kitchen appliances
- bathroom fittings
- outside areas, such as new driveway, garage, paths
- sorting out the garden
- security gates or systems, if deemed necessary
- the pool – or having one built
- transport – if you are not taking your own, will you need to buy a car out there?
- connection charges for the utilities
- insurance for the property.

Remember, too, that you will need to budget for medical and dental services, either private insurance, or at least payments for certain services and medicines (some can be claimed back, but not all).

EQUIPPING AND FURNISHING THE PROPERTY

Furniture, fittings and appliances can all be bought in Portugal – mostly at the large retail parks, hypermarkets and DIY superstores. Cheap goods can be found on the monthly markets, or *feiras*. Smaller, local retail stores will stock other items you will need. Buying locally means you are sure appliances fit and can have them installed if necessary. You also have the benefit of being on-the-spot for dealing with problems or faulty goods. Many consumer 'white goods' and other durables are not always that cheap, but the alternative of having your own shipped out may just not be practical.

ANNUAL RUNNING COSTS

Utilities are not cheap in Portugal. You may expect the following approximate level of prices:

Electricity for a small villa (excluding heating).	£1,600.00 per annum
Bottled gas for cooking/some water heating.	Approx. 15 euros bottle
Mains water, metered, excluding pool.	£800 annum
Telephone.	Subjective of course, but still considered very high, especially regional and international calls.

Other on-going payments may include:

◆ **Council tax rates:** between 0.2 and 0.8% house valuation, 5% for those bought through off-shore companies.

◆ **Community or management fees:** depends on type and size of property and what services are offered. Check you know beforehand what you might be expected to contribute.

◆ **Maintenance of private gardens and pool:** you may be able to hire someone local to do this for you very cheaply, or you may have to call in property manage-ment agents.

SUMMARY

Even if you have already a cash sum waiting eagerly for the right property, in the excitement of finding that dream place, it can be too easy to overlook all the hidden extras which at some point or other will require paying. There is absolutely no point in splashing out on your new property, and finding in the long-term you simply cannot afford to live there after all. Do your homework carefully. Research prices in different areas. Compare costs, fees and services offered by professionals you will need. Try a few shorter-term visits and calculate living costs and daily expenditure. Set down your own budget in detail and be honest with yourself about what you can and cannot afford. When you are satisfied, seek sound advice about your personal circumstances, and let yourself be guided by experienced professionals. Many thousands of people have done it successfully before you, so there is no reason to believe it will not work for you too.

11

Before You Go

In the excitement of preparing for your new life abroad, it can be easy to overlook certain preparations which will make your situation more controllable before you go, and that will help you avoid potential problems once in Portugal. You do want the transition to be as smooth as possible, so a little practical planning beforehand can go a long way to easing your move.

LEARNING THE LANGUAGE

Even if you are moving to a predominantly ex-patriot part of the Algarve, it will pay to learn some of the basics of Portuguese before you get there. Although the Portuguese are extremely tolerant people, and very good at speaking English, it must annoy them, deep down, that the vast majority of visitors don't even learn the common courtesies in their language. Those people who *do* bother to try and say a few words have all commented that the response they receive is immediately warming. Once the Portuguese know you are having a go, and even learning their language, they will take the time to help you. Obviously, the more you can take on board the better, as even in the Algarve there will be situations where you may come across someone with less knowledge of English – particularly older people in small shops, or away from the tourist spots in the country areas.

How much more satisfying it is to be able to pass the time of day with someone in their own lingo. (And you are less likely to ripped off if you can communicate in Portuguese, although this doesn't happen often.) Being able to verify bus and train travel times, check prices, ask the time, tell someone you are unwell, are all occasions when a few phrases will help. But also very important if you are making your life out there is being able to go into a bar, order a drink, and join in at a low level, even everyday chit-chat, for example about the football match everyone is avidly following on the TV above your head!

One chap I spoke to about his experiences from the language aspect, said:

> *'If you do some preparation work beforehand, you feel comfortable enough to understand what is going on, and it gets easier the more times you go through the process.'*

Barbara Baird, from Manchester, delightfully told me:

> *'The language is definitely a problem. We got by initially by using friends as interpreters. Our vocabulary*

has increased enormously, if only in a building context. We have a farm down below us and the old lady often pops up with eggs, bread and farm produce. She doesn't speak English and tells us we need to learn Portuguese. We agree on this, and one day I shall be able to converse in Portuguese with her.'

That should get easier now as Barbara has been coming to my classes, so on her next visit she's going to accept the eggs with a few Portuguese phrases.

So, how can you go about learning some Portuguese before you set off?

- **Join a language class**. If you have time before you move, and have access to a local college (adult college or post-16), there may be classes held, mainly in the evening. Typically these will focus on basic holiday language, and will be an excellent introduction for you. If you have never been to a class like this before don't fear. They are normally great fun. It is rare to find someone who has any previous experience of Portuguese so all the class members are in the same boat, and you will be surprised at how much you pick up even after a couple of weeks.

- **Language books and courses at home**. There is now a growing number of books, many with audio tapes/ CDs, which can be used at home. Pick something at a beginners' level to get going, and try to do a little every day if you can. It is better to aim for 10–15 minutes daily than to try and do a whole hour just once a week.

The drip-drip approach always helps in the long run, and ensures you don't become overwhelmed by it all and lose heart.

◆ **Buy a phrase book.** These are helpful for picking up basic survival phrases, but are aimed mostly at holiday visitors. Still, they are a handy starting point, and will also fit in your bag to take with you. Many now come with a tape or CD, which will help you with pronunciation. If you can't get an audio version, aim for one of the books that give you an approximate guide to how each word is said. Bear in mind, though, that it is just approximate – pronunciation can vary in Portugal as anywhere. The Algarve accent, in particular, can be fairly tricky to understand as the locals cut off the beginnings and endings of words. The word for thank-you – *obrigado,* often just sounds like *briga* in the south.

◆ **Watch the television**. The BBC often run repeats of their successful series *Discovering Portuguese*, made in the late 80s, and their new series *Talk Portuguese*, both of which are a mix of language-learning, culture and glorious scenes of different parts of Portugal. They are normally shown on BBC2 in the 'Learning Zone', between 2–6am. Keep a look out in the TV guide to check when they are on, and if you can, record them so you can use them as many times as you want.

◆ **Tune in to satellite TV.** If you have satellite TV, you may well have access to Portuguese TV, such as the international channel RTPi. Check with your supplier. Some dishes can pick up Brazilian channels, which although sounding rather different, are an introduction to the mighty Brazilian soap opera (*telenovela*) so keenly followed in Portugal.

◆ **Read Portuguese newspapers and magazines.** Either pick some up on your visits to Portugal, or ask friends to send you some. Be sensible about what you try and look at – full-page spreads in newspapers will leave you reaching for the vinho bottle, but a short snippet in a magazine may be manageable.

◆ **Read Portuguese books for children and schools.** These are very useful, and there are some companies who produce bilingual books. One is Mantra Publishing, who do a lovely range of bilingual children's books in many languages, including Portuguese. For their catalogue, telephone 020-8445-5123, or visit their website: *www.mantralingua.com*.

◆ **Buy a UK magazine for the Portuguese.** Another useful source of Portuguese reading matter is the magazine produced for the Portuguese communities in the UK: *Vida Nova*. It costs £15 for 10 editions. Telephone 020-7625-5672 or email: *info@vida-nova.co.uk*.

◆ **Learn on the internet**. There are some internet sites with language-learning facilities, such as the on-line course from Glasgow University '*De tudo um pouco*'. Even without internet access, if you have a computer, you can buy super CD Roms to use on them, with great games and if you have a speaker you can hear the pronunciation of words. EuroTalk (World Talk) have a few in their series. Telephone 0800-018-8838, or visit the website: *www.eurotalk.co.uk*.

Whatever you do will be a good starting point, and win you friends in Portugal. You can continue your efforts once you get there (see also Chapters 13 and 14). Do feel free to contact me for further advice on learning the language, and finding a class near you, by writing to me c/o the Publishers.

PREPARING FOR THE CULTURE SHOCK

Now Portugal is not so markedly different as some countries you could have chosen to head for. As a fully-fledged and active member of the EU, it abides by European rulings, is a democratic country, tolerant, open and free, and welcoming to its many frequent visitors. It is still one of the poorer countries in the EU, although it has benefited over the years from subsidies, a result of which you can see quite clearly in all the new roads and highways improvements carried out. Its economy has been pretty stable for a long time, although it is currently enduring a rougher time domestically.

Since the end of Europe's longest dictatorship in 1974, it has become increasingly forward-thinking. There have been more opportunities, especially for women and in education, and hi-profile foreign investment there is a sign of the outside world's confidence in its workforce and the standards of work there. On the other hand, it is still (thankfully) a country with its traditions, many of these linked to religious beliefs, a country where the family is still important, and where people are still prepared to help each other for no gain other than the satisfaction of being a good citizen. And that is particularly manifest in the rural areas, of which Portugal has a large spread.

You may think that if you are going to spend your life surrounded by mostly ex-patriot colleagues in the south you have no need to consider what might be different about the Portuguese way of life. But that would be to discount the possibility of branching out beyond the G&T soirées and getting to grips with the real culture of your newly adopted land. If you are travelling to areas outside the realm of the southern coast, you will, inevitably, confront the real thing. So, what might be different?

- A slower approach to life – there's always another day.

- Slower service in shops and offices.

- Red-tape and form-filling.

- Working hours – shops usually close for a couple of hours in the middle of the day, then open into the evening.

- Business – long lunches, etiquette, polite forms of address, smart suits.

- Children often out late, promenading with families, in restaurants.

- Many people eat lunch out.

- No 'last orders', but equally, fewer drink-related problems.

- Food, drink, café-culture.

- Leisure – fewer public leisure centres than in UK.

- Activities – few opportunities for evening classes.

- Shops – apart from large cities, range is usually much smaller, a lot of shopping done in small, local businesses and at the market.

- Pets – not a Portuguese tradition, although some keep small dogs, or birds in cages. In rural areas dogs are kept chained up as guard dogs. There is little feeling of sentiment towards animals, although the street dogs in the Algarve are well-fed, often by butchers.

- Driving – can be a problem! See next chapter.

So, what can you do to lessen any 'culture shock' in advance of your trip? The main thing to do is to learn as much about Portugal and its people before you go. There are suggestions on page 217, for useful books. Many good travel guides include sections on Portuguese customs and way of life. The BBC TV series mentioned earlier will also give you a flavour of what is awaiting you. Check out the internet if you have access. You could start with the following general sites:

www.portugal-insite.pt
www.portugalvirtual.pt
www.interacesso.pt/lugares/portnet/htm
www.portugal-info.net
www.portugal.org
www.icep.pt

Nicki Grihault, author of *Working in Asia* (In Print Publishing) says it can take about a year to really settle into a new culture, at which point you should be able to enjoy the positive aspects of the new environment and accept the differences for what they are. The most important thing to remember is to keep an open mind about your soon-to-be new host country. It is not too different an environment to settle into, and if you take on board at least some of the local ways and customs, not only will it ingratiate you with the people there, but you may just find you enjoy your stay there that little bit more.

DECIDING WHETHER TO LET OR SELL YOUR UK HOME

The biggest logistical problem people are generally faced with is what to do with property they own in the UK. Should you keep your property and rent it out whilst you're away, or is your move on such a permanent level that you want to sell it? Do you have family commitments to take into account, or are you in a relatively independent situation?

Keeping hold of your property and renting it out in your absence is an option that allows you a base to come home to. But how do you overcome the much-highlighted problem of nightmare tenants? Unfortunately, the only way you can guarantee your home will be looked after is to rent it to family or good friends you can trust. Even here you can never be too sure, and sometimes it is far more difficult to be heavy-handed with people you know well. Going through a letting agency does not always assure reliable people, despite claims of vetting of prospective tenants. The most professional and seemingly charming people can change totally once they are inside your property. Of course, not *every* tenant will turn into a problem, and in the end you have to rely on instinct when you meet them, and of course luck.

LETTING AGENCIES

An agent undertakes to oversee the whole letting process for you, including:

♦ advertising the house
♦ vetting tenants
♦ entering into contract with them
♦ collecting rent,

and generally sorting out any problems when you are away. In return, they usually request a fee in the form of a percentage of the rent (typically around 10%). You may feel this is a lot out of your rental income, but if you have no one who can keep a check on the house, collect rent, or get repairs done for you, it may be your only option.

LETTING YOURSELF

If you choose to let yourself set your required rental income, based on the going local rate (see your local paper and check letting and housing agents), and what you need to cover your mortgage payments. If advertising yourself, make sure you state clearly the profile of the person you are looking for: professional/sex/smokers or not/pets... When showing people around the house try to get a feel for the kind of person they appear to be. Don't necessarily accept the first potential tenant who comes along, unless you really feel sure they would be suitable. Ask for references from previous landlords, employers and even banks, and follow up with a couple of phone-calls if you are in any doubt. Be clear about how long the let is for. Contracts should be Assured short-hold tenancy types, which only allow an initial let of six months and which can then be renewed if required. These give you a safer possibility of evicting bad tenants. Also clearly state what bills the tenant must pay, and any other relevant house rules. Take a deposit (usually 1–3 months' rent), which is only refundable at the end of the tenancy, provided there has been no damage, and that all bills have been paid. Remove anything of value and put in storage if you cannot leave it with family or friends.

SELLING YOUR HOUSE

If you are making a definitive move and want to sell property, seek guidance from local property agents. You can do the advertising and selling yourself, but you will need some legal guidance when it comes to exchanging contracts. Much of the rest of the process you could handle yourself if you wanted to. Recently-established websites allow people to sell homes on the net. Check out *Buying & Selling Your House* by Adam Walker for further insight.

MOVING THE FURNITURE

If you have decided on a definite move your next thoughts should include what amount of your own household goods you wish to take with you. Of course, if you only intend to move on a semi-permanent basis, perhaps retaining property to which you will return at a later date, then perhaps you only require your 'favourite' pieces of furniture removing. You may need expert help and advice in packing goods specifically for transportation abroad, especially if any are being sent by boat or air-freight. A good removals firm will carry this out, using specialist packing materials if necessary. If you are packing yourself, remember to use items such as blankets and cushions as padded space-fillers around other items. A complete house removal may cost on average £5000. Further details can be obtained from any of the removal firms listed at the end of this book. Ask for details of their insurance claims record to verify how good their standards are.

BEFORE YOU LEAVE

You will probably need to acquire a **Baggage certificate**, **Inventory** and **Affidavit**. To obtain a Baggage Certificate, you need to produce copies of your overseas property deeds (notarised) or a resident's permit, both within 90 days of issue. The Baggage Certificate will allow you duty-free importation of any of your personal belongings, provided they have been used by you for at least six months prior to moving. You will also need a duplicated inventory (translated), which should include details of main items, and smaller or loose items and electricals (include make and serial number). In the case of recently acquired electricals, keep receipts and guarantees with you.

Send all these documents to the relevant Consulate, from where your baggage certificate will be issued. Again, you will have up to 90 days in which to use it. If you have any doubts at all, contact the Consulate well in advance of your move for their latest advice. If you are using a removals firm to transport your goods, they will do all the necessary paperwork on your behalf. It is important, then, to use a company with either offices in Portugal, or one which has experience in dealing with Portuguese affairs.

You could try:

Overs International, Tel: 01252-343 646/*www.overs.co.uk*
Trans-Portugal European Ltd, Tel: 020-7403 1440/
  www.trans-portugal.com
The Old House (Removals and Warehousing), Tel: 01323-
  892 204/*www.amsmoving.co.uk*

For detailed guidance on importing goods: Lisbon
Customs and Excise – Direcção Geral das Alfândegas,
Rua da Alfândega, 1100 – 016 Lisboa. Tel: 21-881-3700/
Email: *dgaiec@dgaiec.min-financas.pt*.

More suggestions in the Directory, or check with firms
local to you.

Glossary of furniture vocabulary

bed	*cama*
wardrobe	*guarda-roupa*
dressing table	*toucador*
bookcase	*estante*
chair	*cadeira*
arm chair	*poltrona*
table	*mesa*
sofa/settee	*sofá*
sideboard/cupboard	*aparador/armário*
TV set	*televisor*
video	*gravador de vídeo*
hi-fi equipment	*aparelho de som/ hi-fi*
radio	*rádio*
computer	*computador*
desk	*secretária*

dresser	*louceiro*
washing machine	*máquina de lavar roupa*
microwave	*micro-ondas*
dishwasher	*máquina de lavar louça*
fridge	*frigorífico*
cooker	*fogão*
vacuum cleaner	*aspirador*
freezer	*congelador*
books	*livros*
clothes	*roupa*
toys	*brinquedos*
pottery/ornaments	*bibelôs*
crockery	*louça*
cutlery	*talheres*
hairdryer	*secador de cabelo*
electric shaver	*máquina de barbear*
CD/tape player	*gravador/leitor de CD*
kettle	*chaleira*
camera	*máquina fotográfica*
iron	*ferro*

FAMILY AND PETS

If you wish to take any pets with you to Portugal, they must be checked by a UK vet and initially given a clean bill of health, have inoculations up to date, and be issued with a vet's certificate to travel (*atestado sanitário*). This must be translated into Portuguese and presented to the Portuguese authorities on arrival. Rabies is still clear from Portugal, and they are keen to let it stay that way. Your certificate must state that your animal comes from a Rabies-free area.

If you are travelling down through France and Spain yourself with your animal, beware that it is still possible for rabies to be contracted in rural areas, so do not let your animal wander off in wooded areas. Your own vet will be able to issue you with all the necessary guidance to enable your pet to travel. You need to start planning this all well in advance of your intended journey – at least six months, in order for all vaccines and paperwork to go through. For absolute advice, contact Department of Environment, Food and Rural Affairs, 1A Page Street, London SW1P 4PQ. Tel: 0207-904-6346/7.

FAMILY CONSIDERATIONS

For some people the decision to move abroad can be all-pervading, and sometimes the over-riding excitement and anticipation needs to be tempered with consideration of how the move may affect other family members.

PARENTS

Whether or not you now live at home with your parents, you may need to assure them that you will take a sensible approach to your move, and that you have a secure place to travel to. Sharing details of your intended location with them may help to alleviate some of the uncertainties about where you are off to. You may be able to arrange for them, or other family members, to visit you at some point, so they can see for themselves where you are. Whilst you are abroad make regular contact with your family, to keep them positive about what you are doing.

SPOUSE AND CHILDREN

If your decision to move away involves uprooting your whole family, there are far more considerations to take into account:

- ◆ What will your spouse do for a living?
- ◆ Schooling for children?
- ◆ Fitting into a new lifestyle/culture?
- ◆ Taking your family away from friends and familiarity.
- ◆ Finding suitable accommodation.
- ◆ Coping if things go wrong.

Many families each year make the move to warmer climes, Portugal included. The allure of a more clement climate, and gentler way of life is an extremely strong force. However, problems do arise when one partner finds him or herself without work. Frustration, anger, depression can all intrude on family life, and great numbers of ex-patriot hopefuls too quickly succumb to the cheap booze available at all hours in many countries. All too soon life can spiral downwards, affecting the whole family in a disastrous way. Families break up at alarming rates in typical ex-pat hotspots. So what can you do to avoid these problems from the start?

- ◆ Discuss with the whole family before you leave what changes are likely to occur and how you will all deal with them.

- ◆ Explore the possibilities of work for your spouse – what skills can be built on?

- ◆ Ensure you do things together as a family, so that no-one feels neglected. This can be particularly rewarding if you take up an activity involving you in the local community (church, language classes, sport, travel).

Try to take enough money with you to tide you over the first few months until work is providing you with a living, or until salary or pension payments start coming through regularly. You may have to live frugally for a while, but allow small treats for the family to keep up morale. Although a move abroad can be exciting for everyone, it can also be bewildering and hard-work. Plan in advance to soften the low points. For more thoughts on these issues, try the Culture Shock! guides from Kuperard press, particularly 'A parent's guide' and 'A wife's guide'.

GROWN-UP CHILDREN

You may be at a point in life where your children have already left home, and you have decided to fly the nest yourself. Children can react in two very distinct ways. Either they will be extremely supportive and think what you are doing is great, or they'll respond with incredulity and wonder what on earth you're up to! This can be a signal of various emotions:

- Their secure life is suddenly being shaken – parents don't move away from their children.

- What is going to happen to the family home? There'll be no place to drop in on any more.

- How will they contact you when they have problems or need some cash?

You may need to reassure them about your plans, but after all if this is something you really want to do, who should stand in your way? Try to turn their concerns into positives. They will be able to visit regularly and can keep in touch by email.

MAKING TRAVEL ARRANGEMENTS

Having made the decision to get up and go, your next move will be to consider how to get yourself and (possibly) your belongings over the waters, and this obviously depends very much on your intentions:

- How long will your stay be?
    - Is this your definitive trip there?
    - Is it an exploratory trip?

- How much will you need with you initially?
    - Clothes and personal items.
    - Furniture.

- Will you need a car with you?

- Are you working to a budget?

- Your exact destination
    - north/south
    - coast/inland.

- Are you travelling alone/with family?

TRAVELLING BY AIR

This is by far the quickest, most efficient way to travel, especially if you have little baggage. Flights are available either through your local travel agencies, or contact the airlines direct. You can also check out some of the latest cheap deals on the internet.

www.travelocity.co.uk
www.travelselect.com
www.travelstore.com
www.uTravel.co.uk

www.easyjet.com
www.go-fly.com
www.ryanair.com

Telephone airlines direct, especially for flights to Lisbon. Amongst others:

TAP (Portuguese airlines)	0845-601-0932
BA	0845-773-3377
SwissAir	0845-601-0956
Lufthansa	0845-773-7747
KLM	0870-507-4074
Portugalia	0870-755-0025 (from Manchester)

Equally so, on offer over the winter are cheap long-stay holidays, designed for those people wishing to escape the British winter blues, but certainly affording an ideal opportunity to reach destinations in sunnier climes. They provide good, cheap accommodation in large hotel complexes whilst you look around for alternatives. I chose this option on one visit to the Algarve, and ended up paying the equivalent of about £25 a week for a lovely apartment, including gas, water and electricity, over the winter until I moved on.

TAKING A FERRY

If you are taking your car, you have a number of alternative boat routes:

◆ To a French port such as St Malo, Calais or Caen, amongst others, (via Channel ferry) and drive on, or to

Santander or Bilbao, N. Spain: 24 hour crossing and drive on.

Contact Brittany Ferries (Santander or via France). Tel 0990-360 360.
P&O Ferries (for Bilbao). Tel: 0990-980980. The latest leaflet will be available from travel agents.

Costs vary according to season, number of passengers travelling in vehicle, size of vehicle, but allow enough in your budget, especially if driving through France, as you will need overnight accommodation too.

TRAINS AND COACHES

A great journey for the more adventurous is by train. Take Eurostar from London to Paris and then a train to Lisbon and connections. Alternatively, catch a National Express coach from London Victoria. Long journeys (approx. 1½–2 days), but relatively cheap and interesting, although coach is uncomfortable during the night.

Details

Eurostar – Waterloo Station, London, and all main BR stations. Tel: 01233-617575.
Le Shuttle: 0990-353535.
BR Continental Section, Victoria Station, London SW1. Tel: 020-7834-2345.
National Express coaches (Eurolines), Victoria Coach Station, Buckingham Palace Rd, London SW1. Tel: 020-7730-0202.

SUMMARY

Sorting out your new life abroad isn't just about the house

and place you'll be living in. It's also about the planning for that new life, preparing for what you might encounter, settling affairs in the UK, and having contingency plans in hand for whatever may be thrown up. Have you:

- started to learn the language?

- read up about Portugal and its people and customs?

- made a decision about your UK property and looked into the best way to either sell or let?

- enquired about removals and checked a few companies?

- seen your vet about your pet travelling?

- talked everything through with family members?

- checked out all the most efficient ways of getting there?

12

Portuguese Systems

In order to enjoy your new life to the full, whether that be just for part of the year, or permanently, you may need to know how the Portuguese systems for motoring, health, finance, and education work, as well as having a good idea of what to do when dealing with the law, and tax issues. One of the best sources of up-to-date information on these aspects is **AFPOP** (Association of Foreign Property Owners of Portugal), who regularly publish info bulletins and update magazines. They can be contacted at: AFPOP, Apartado 728, 8501-917 Portimão, Algarve, Portugal/Tel: 282-458-509/Email: *afpop@ip.pt*.

Guidance and information sheets are also available from the Portuguese Consulates in the UK. You should always check with them on major aspects of your move to

Portugal, for the latest advice, as laws, and especially EU directives, are a fluid commodity.

APPLYING FOR RESIDENCE

One of the first things you will need to do is to apply for a residence card (*residência*), which gives you the right to live in Portugal for specific lengths of time. EU citizens no longer need a residence visa before they travel to Portugal, so everything can be done once you are there. The Portuguese Immigration Service (*Serviço de Estrangeiros e Fronteiras* – SEF) are the people who deal with this. They have offices in Lisbon, Coimbra, Porto, Faro, Portimão, Ponta Delgada and Funchal (Madeira).

The table on the next page is an overview of what type of permit is required by different people:

NB. Wage earners no longer require a work permit in Portugal; they are treated as equals with their Portuguese counterparts, but they must have a formal work contract as proof of their work.

Rules governing non-EU members are slightly different, as they will require a residence visa issued by the Portuguese consulate in their own country.

When you go to apply for your permit, have with you as much information and documentation as possible to start with, including proof of income, or work contracts. You will be required to fill in various forms (this is where your love-affair with Portuguese bureaucracy really begins!),

Situation	Type of permit	Valid
Working in Portugal for no longer than 3 months.	No permit required.	n/a
Seasonal worker – work period no longer than 8 months.	No permit required.	n/a
Working for more than three, but less than 12 months.	Temporary residence permit.	Valid for duration of work contract/can be extended beyond one year and new permit will be valid for 5 years.
Working for more than one year.	Residence permit.	5 years, renewable for 10 years.
Providing a service, with set duration of work.	Temporary permit.	Can be renewed on application, if work extended.
Self-employed people.	Residence permit.	5 years, renewable for 10.
Persons of independent means, including the retired.	Residence permit, granted if: they can show they have sufficient income to support themselves and families without state assistance/they have health cover (see later) – if not in receipt of state pension, must have private medical insurance.	Two years in the first instance, renewable for five years.
Spouse of someone working.	Residence permit granted.	Same as main applicant.
Children under 14.	Residence granted and endorsed on parents' permit, provided one of parents has been granted full residence.	Same as parents.

and may be asked for specific pieces of documentation. Make sure you have a number of copies of vital pieces of paper before you get out there, so that you speed up the process, and you keep a check on where your documentation is. It is probably worth starting to build up a relevant file before you leave. You could include copies of:

- passport pages
- bank statements
- medical notes
- pet notes
- work contract/ letter
- pension details
- insurance
- motoring info (see next section)
- letters of introduction from any Portuguese people/ companies
- any relevant documents in translation
- birth/marriage certificates
- salary receipts/proof of own business
- school registration documents for children
- multiple passport-type photos of each member of the family.

MOTORING REQUIREMENTS

Driving can be a hair-raising experience in Portugal, as most people will tell you who have done it. It is not in jest that the Portuguese are labelled some of the worst drivers in Europe – the incidence of road-related accidents and fatalities is horrendously high (Portugal has more car accidents than any other European country). Although many roads and highways are now wonderfully sleek, thanks to huge investment in infrastructure in the last 5 years, some of the roads are no more than pit-holed bumpy tracks, which are fine if you are merely ambling along with your donkey and a herd of goats, but get on it with your latest sporty number, and it won't be long before you're heading for the *oficina de reparos*.

Not only that, but Portuguese drivers seem to have an impending sense of meeting their maker whilst out on the roads – at least it would appear so to anyone else who has to suffer their overtaking on blind bends, bumper-bumping close behind you, and even drink-driving, which, despite the many campaigns and zero-tolerance, is still prevalent, and amongst a fair number of ex-patriots too. However, if you are going to be a frequent, or long-term resident there, unless you base yourself right in the middle of a town centre, it is likely you will need to use a vehicle at some point or other.

IMPORTING CARS

A vehicle can be imported duty-free from the UK, provided you have been resident there before moving to Portugal, and as long as the car is up to date with its tax. The process can be horrendous and tax and fees exorbitant. Most residents agree that it is far easier and cheaper to buy a car in Portugal. Many are advertised in the English-speaking publications. Second-hand cars bought out there also tend to suffer less from rust than in northern Europe. It is also safer to buy a left-hand drive car to avoid problems on the road once out and about.

DRIVING LICENCE

If you still have an old-style (green) licence, that must be exchanged for a Portuguese-issued licence as soon as you intend to drive in Portugal. If you have one of the new-style EU (pink) licences, you can drive on that until it expires; then you will have to apply for a Portuguese one, if Portugal is to be your main or permanent home. In order to acquire a Portuguese licence you have to take (and pass) a driving test there. The local Licensing Offices will give you further details: *Direcção Geral de Viação*.

The British Embassy in Lisbon cites two very valid reasons why it is important, in the long-run, to have a Portuguese licence:

◆ The address on the licence must be the valid address of the licence-holder – this is as legally binding as in the UK.

◆ Licences which may need replacing (lost or stolen) can only be replaced by the issuing authority; the DVLA will not issue replacement licences to an overseas address.

LAWS OF THE ROAD

It is important to remember that driving is on the right in Portugal, and priority given to the right, especially important on roundabouts. Always carry with you any documents relevant to the vehicle:

◆ registration documents
◆ insurance
◆ licence

- tax/MOT certificates if applicable
- letter of authority if driving someone else's car.

The GNR Traffic police can be real sticklers for detail, and often seek out foreign-registered cars for attention. There are a number of toll roads now in Portugal, on the major highways, and an innovative scheme, called *Via Verde*, allows those drivers set up with a special account, to 'swipe' themselves through an automatic toll machine. Only drive in that lane if you have the account.

Most driving signs are the same as anywhere – the symbols are fairly universal. The Collins *Portuguese Survival Guide* has a number of useful pages dedicated to driving signs and symbols. Seatbelts are compulsory, there is zero-tolerance on drinking, and speed limits are 50kph (30mph) in built-up areas, 90kph (56mph) on open roads and 120kph (74mph) on motorways.

The Portuguese AA, Automóvel Club de Portugal (ACP), has a range of maps, booklets and advice: Head Office: Rua Rosa Araújo 24/6, 1250 Lisboa. Tel: 21-396-3931/ *www.acp.pt.*

AFPOP have a comprehensive guide to driving in Portugal, plus update sheets as laws are amended.

THE HEALTH SYSTEM

The quality of services provided under the health system in Portugal can be very hit and miss, and often where you live will dictate what facilities you have within reach and how good their resources are (sounds vaguely familiar, this?). Portugal spends 7.9% of its GDP on Health, compared with 6.8 in the UK and 13.9 in the USA. The health system is run by the *Ministério da Saúde*, through a series of local centres – administrative (*administração regional de saúde*) and the health centres (*centros de saúde*). Most local hospitals are small and outdated, and some towns only have a *centro de saúde*, which cannot possibly cover all treatments, thereby necessitating transfers of ill people to the nearest suitable location. However, the number of hospital beds in the country is not too different from other 'advanced' countries; you are just as likely to get a bed in Portugal, with 4.1 beds per 1000 people, as you are in the UK (4.5 beds).

Comments from residents reflect the arbitrary nature of the quality of care:

> *'The Health System is very good.'*

> *'I had to see a doctor once and it was OK.'*

> *'Beware of Portuguese hospitals and repatriate yourself if you can!'*

> *'We used the health system on our first visit when I sustained broken toes. It all worked extremely well, with minimal cost. Very impressed with both the local Centro de Saúde in Silves and Portimão hospital.'*

> *'Private treatment preferable if you can afford it, or the insurance premiums. State system improving. Foreign staff used a lot. Doctors are good, but nursing can be appalling: insensitive, no communication. In Lagos state hospital it is possible to be put in a room to yourself or*

share with one other person for the price of a medium-standard hotel.'

...and this wonderful description of how confusing it can all get...

'We recently registered with our local doctor. If you need to visit him you can either make a private appointment in the afternoon (40 euros) or join the queue at 8am at the surgery, where he sees a set number of patients and you are given a number (like at the supermarket) when you go in. When the numbers given out reach his maximum for his time constraints that morning patients are automatically switched to see the nurse. This happened to us, but the nurse didn't turn up because her baby was ill and because we didn't understand what was being said, we waited from 8 until 11.40am without seeing anyone.'

As for actual access to the system, non-resident visitors and holidaymakers can have free emergency treatment if they show their passport and E111 form, available from UK Post Offices, and valid for life. For British people who have taken up residency in Portugal, entitlement to the health service is the same as for Portuguese nationals. However, in order to become part of the system in the first place, you have to apply for your National Insurance Card (*Cartão de Utente*) at the local health centre. You need to show your passport, and residence permit. Until the card has been issued, you will only be entitled to free treatment in an emergency.

Retired people receiving UK state pensions can apply for an NHS card and enrol with a Portuguese state GP just with their passport and receipts from pension payments. For more on pensions, see later.

Even within the state health system, many people still have to pay for consultations with GPs, and medicines. These can be claimed back against tax, but many foreign residents decide to take out their own, private medical insurance in any case, so that they have access to any number of private clinics (certainly in the south). In other parts of Portugal, you may need to rely more on the national system than elsewhere. Private clinics are, otherwise, extremely expensive.

See Directory for companies providing private medical insurance.

Serviços de Emergencia – Emergency Services
Portugal benefits from an excellent national emergency service, operating in Portuguese, French and English. The Number 112 gives access to *polícia, hospital, serviço de ambulâncias* or *bombeiros*.

ALTERNATIVE MEDICINE

Alternative forms of treatment, such as homeopathy, aromatherapy and the likes, have been slow to take off in Portugal, although there have always been *curandeiros* and *ervanários* (healers and herbalists). There are some practitioners in Lisbon, and the Algarve has a number of mainly foreign-led services. Perhaps it is viewed as too 'New Age' for this still conservative people, which is surprising given the pagan-like practices still carried out in some northern rural towns, where the local '*curandeira*' may be called on to cure sickness.

EDUCATION

In Portugal, compulsory education is free, and pupils in cases of hardship also receive free books, transport, meals and, sometimes, accommodation. However at secondary level token tuition fees are charged and books must be purchased. Most pupils attend state-run schools, but a number may choose to go to a private institution which receives equal benefits as state schools if it follows the same national curriculum.

Compulsory education is divided into 3 *ciclos*, corresponding to primary (taught in an *escola primária*), preparatory (*escola preparatória* or *secundária* – up to age 12), and the third *ciclo*, up to school leaving age at 15. Throughout this time Portuguese youngsters are taught a range of subjects, including one or two foreign languages, personal and social education. Many schools operate a 'shift' system to their timetable, as resources can only allow pupils to attend either in the mornings or afternoons. Some may attend school in the evening. Vocational schools were set up in 1989 as a practical alternative to normal secondary schooling, most offering 3-year courses leading to vocational qualifications, and specialist art schools exist for people wishing to enter the worlds of dance, music, or the visual arts.

In general, Portuguese schools are very like other countries' – though the vast majority are in modern buildings, often lacking in inspiration. Pupils do not wear uniform apart from at some private, or church-run schools. Most children eat in the school *refeitório*.

For more info on the Portuguese school system, and on further and higher education possibilities, see the following websites:

www.min-edu.pt
www.deb.min-edu.pt
www.desup.min-edu.pt

INTERNATIONAL SCHOOLS

There is a growing number of International Schools in Portugal, reflecting the increasing numbers of foreign residents. Some of these follow a British or American curriculum, but others also cater for the Portuguese market, with a dual system in place. They benefit, in most cases, from enhanced facilities, and an interesting mix of nationalities. Some, such as the Oporto British School, St Dominic's in Lisbon, or the International School of the Algarve at Porches, are long-established, reputable schools. However, there have been reported cases of establishments run by fraudsters, especially in the Algarve, where businesses can appear and disappear in the bat of a sunburnt eyelid! It is important to check each establishment carefully, asking for its school brochure, details of the curriculum, its teachers, and facilities. Make sure you visit any potential school, and talk to other parents if you can. The following schools are recommended:

SCHOOL	AGE
Algarve International School Porches, Lagoa Tel: 282-342547/8	4–16
Barlavento English School Lagos Tel: 282-789206	4–11
Colégio Internacional de Vilamoura Vilamoura Tel: 289-321585	4–18
Escola Internacional de S.Lourenço Almancil Tel: 289-398328	3–16
St Julian's School Carcavelos (Lisbon) Tel: 21-4570140	3–18
St Dominic's College Parede (Lisbon) Tel: 21-4440434	4–16
St George's School Cascais Tel: 21-4840555	3–13
Queen Elizabeth's School Alvalade (Lisbon) Tel: 21-8486928	3–11
Oporto British School Porto Tel: 22-6166660	3–18
CLIP Oporto International School (Lower and Upper) Porto Tel: 22-6186790	6–18
CLIC Colégio Luso Internacional do Centro Marinha Grande Tel: 244-503710	5–18
British School Funchal (Madeira) Tel: 291-773218	4–10

DEALING WITH YOUR FINANCES

One thing you will need to do as soon as possible, is to check you have all your financial matters in hand. If you are going through the process of buying property, this is something which will be an important feature of the process, and you should be receiving sound advice from your advisors. It is worth keeping contact with a good financial advisor, unless your finances are very straight-forward to keep reins on.

Bank accounts

Portugal is a full member of the euro-zone and all transactions are now in the euro, although prices are still also given in *escudos* in many shops, restaurants and on bills. It is possible to open a bank account in euros or other foreign currency, whether as a resident or just a visitor, and there is no restriction on the amount of money passing into and out of the country.

Banks generally open from 8.30 until 3pm, sometimes longer in tourist areas, Monday to Friday only. The system of ATMs, called *Multibancos*, is extensive through-out the country. You can use these to withdraw or deposit cash, pay bills, and check accounts. Most Portuguese banks are now very modern, efficient and use the latest technology, including internet banking. It is worth building up a good relationship with your bank's personnel, especially the *gerente* (manager). I know one couple whose bank manager rang them in the UK to let them know their account was running low and their next direct debits might not be covered. As you can be in hot water in Portugal for not honouring cheque payments, that was an extremely good relationship to have established.

You can open either a current (cheque) account – *conta corrente*, or deposit account – *depósito a prazo*. You have to be over 18, and will need ID and your tax (fiscal) card. It is worth keeping an account open in the UK too, especially if you are dividing your time between the two.

TAX ISSUES

Anyone deemed resident in Portugal will pay taxes to the Portuguese authorities. If you live in Portugal for over 183 days in any calendar year, or you have a permanent home there, you are considered a resident of Portugal. Otherwise, you continue to pay UK taxes. There is an agreement in place to avoid people paying double taxation, but you need to establish to which authorities you will be liable. If you are paying in Portugal, you need a fiscal card with a tax number (*número de contribuinte*), from the local tax office (*Repartição das Finanças*). If you have bought property in Portugal you will already have one of these.

Taxpayers have to submit their own tax returns in Portugal:

(a) Between 1 February and 15 March for earnings from employment and/or pensions.
(b) Between 16 March and 30 April for all other income.

Tax rates range from 14–40%, and there is a whole list of possible deductions you can make, including certain health payments and education. However, as financial regulations often change, you need to make sure your information is the very latest before you fill in the forms. You can get help from the local tax offices or a reputable firm of accountants. The Portuguese tax system website has information in English on: *www.dgci.min-financas.pt.*

You can also get advice from the UK's Inland Revenue, via your own office, or on the website: *www.inlandreve-nue.gov.uk.*

MAKING A WILL

You may have not considered yet whether you felt it necessary to make a will, many people leave it later in life, but if you are buying property in Portugal, it is essential to think about this carefully, as you could save a lot of time, cost and effort by having a will made in Portuguese. Although an English will is accepted in Portugal, it needs to be validated by being professionally translated, notarised and authenticated. A will made in Portugal dealing with your property there makes the whole process of sorting out estates in the case of death far easier and reduces the stress of having to run around getting documents translated in the wake of what is usually a difficult time anyway. You may wish to contact one of the listed solicitors in the Directory to find out more about the best way forward for you. Ask other people you know, too, what they have done and whether they can recommend solicitors to you.

BENEFITS AND PENSIONS

With the EU legislation for payments of monies to EU

citizens wherever they happen to be residing within the Union, you can continue to receive your state pension, or benefits whilst you are in Portugal. This also includes UK widows' benefits, unemployment benefit, and maternity benefits. It is best to check first with your nearest UK Social Security/Benefits office for advice about your own situation, and to ensure you have all the relevant paperwork relating to your own claims. The following booklets are of use and are available from the Benefits Agency:

◆ A guide to retirement pensions booklet NP46.
◆ Social Security abroad booklet NI 38.
◆ Your social security insurance, benefits and health care rights in the European Community leaflet SA29.

THE POLICE AND LAW

The vast majority of crimes in Portugal involve the bouncing of cheques (which in itself can lead to virtual expulsion from your bank), and theft. Serious traffic offences account for around 2,500 cases a year, and drug-related crime (theft and assault) has now found its place in an otherwise relatively safe country. The types of heinous crimes (sexual, against children, shootings) which sadly have become the norm in the UK, USA and elsewhere, are still very rare in Portugal.

Common contravention of the law at a less serious level usually involves traffic-related offences (particularly parking). These are usually simply dealt with by an on-the-spot fine payable at the local police station (*esquadra*). The police are usually immune to excuses, and fines can be pretty hefty.

Every citizen has the right of access to the judicial system, as laid down by the Constitution. Courts are autonomous and are bound only to the law of the land and the demands of the Constitution.

Supreme Court
The High Court – sits in Lisbon,
can judge on civil, criminal, commercial cases

Courts of Secondary Jurisdiction
Act as Courts of Appeal. Cases over a certain limit
can appeal to the Supreme Court

Courts of Primary Jurisdiction

County Courts	**Admin Courts**	**Tax Courts**
General cases, criminal, family, minors, labour cases. Court's decision final in cases under a certain value. Over this threshold you can appeal to the Courts of Secondary Jurisdiction.	Local and national government matters	Tax cases

There are a number of police forces in Portugal: the *Guarda Nacional Republicana*, (GNR), and the public security police, *Polícia de Segurança Pública* (PSP), both with almost equal numbers of employees. The GNR are quite austere-looking, in grey uniforms, and are military-led. The PSP wear dark blue uniforms, are armed (as are their GNR counterparts), and deal with general policing matters, and traffic. There is also the *Polícia Judiciária* (Criminal Investigation Unit), *Brigada de Trânsito* (Traffic

Brigade), *Guarda Fiscal* (Customs and Excise patrols) and the *Polícia Marítima* (Coastguard).

If you find yourself in trouble with the police and you are not sure what to do, take a Portuguese-speaking person with you to the police station. It may be something fairly routine, such as needing to verify documents, or you may need further intervention. In serious cases, you may be advised to contact the nearest British Consulate for further advice. (See Directory). For general information on citizens' rights, see: *www.infocid.pt*

SUMMARY

Although at first the aspect of getting set up with all the correct paperwork and systems in place may seem quite daunting, if you attack the process systematically and calmly, seeking necessary guidance from relevant authorities in advance, you will eventually have things sorted.

Have you:

- checked your position about residence?

- built up a useful file of documents in advance?

- decided on what to do about a vehicle?

- got the appropriate driving documents and insurance in place?

- got relevant medical paperwork, private cover, or applied for an NHS card?

- located your local health centres and surgeries?

- found information about local schools?

- considered the Portuguese or International education system?

- explored some banks and made a decision about accounts?

- sorted out your tax position?

- sought advice on making a will?

- contacted the relevant authorities about transferring payments of pensions and benefits?

Daily Life in Portugal

So, what is life in Portugal like, on a day-to-day basis? Will your routines be any different? How will you manage everyday domestic situations, and deal with those vital aspects of life as we know it, such as paying your 'leccy bill, having mail delivered, making a phone call (if you can get a phone connected), or deciding whether or not you can survive without pie and chips or late-night Chinese take-aways!

THE COST OF LIVING

It has always been cheaper to do most things in Portugal than in the UK, especially in relation to food, drink, public transport and accommodation. Since the introduction of the euro (to which Portugal was one of the first countries to sign up), without a doubt, and according to consensus, prices have been rising. As elsewhere in the

EU, the new currency allowed those with enough savvy to outwit unsuspecting tourists by rounding up figures, and increasing their prices beyond a normal annual incline. Of course, it is not just tourists who are affected, but in the Algarve it is more noticeable in the restaurants and bars.

Away from hotspots it is still possible to eat, drink and be merry for a fraction of what it would cost you back home, and even where prices have gone up, as a visitor it is still a relatively cheap destination. However, for longer-term residents, the picture may not appear quite as rosy, as many people have commented that it is definitely not as cheap as it used to be, all things taken into account. With the Portuguese economy also in flux right now, even the Portuguese have been feeling the pinch. One article in the AFPOP newsletter I recently read, pointed out how much cheaper many items were in Spanish supermarkets; for those near enough to the border to get across without spending too much on petrol, the trip looked worthwhile.

UTILITIES

Electricity

The voltage in Portugal is 220V, with round 2-pin plugs. You will need to replace UK plugs on any appliances you take with you, or better still, simply buy them once you are there. If you are renting accommodation, make sure you have the meter read before you move in, and keep an on-going note of the usage yourself. In any case, you will need to let the local EDP office (*Electricidade de Portugal*) know that you are the new tenant or owner of the property so that bills can go out in your name. You will need proof of ID and occupancy of the property.

You will receive a monthly bill (*factura*) which outlines what has been used and the amount to pay; it is usually estimated until the meter is read. You can pay by cash over the counter at the EDP office, or once you are sorted out with a bank account, you can pay via the Multibanco cash machines. In rural areas many people have to rely on generators. Even if your property does not need one, it is worth investing in one anyway, in case power is cut – often the case in rainy weather. Electricity is not cheap, but it is often the main source of power. The EDP company has its own website: *www.edp.pt*.

Gas

Piped gas is still not in plentiful supply in Portugal. Most households rely on bottles for both cooking and heating purposes. You can buy them at petrol stations and shops displaying the *Gás* sign, and delivery can be arranged. Normally you pay a deposit for the first bottle, then just pay for each new bottle as you take the empty one back. If you are unfamiliar with how to fit a bottle, ask for someone to show you properly, and see it working. If your water is also heated by bottled gas, when the hot taps are opened, you will hear a whooshing sound as the gas rushes to heat the water. This is normal, but if you smell gas at any time, switch everything off and seek help.

Water

Most, but not all, houses are connected to mains water. If you are, you need to contact the Town Hall (*Câmara Municipal*) to get the account put in your name, taking with you proof of ID plus occupancy of the property. You also pay your bills there, or via a bank account. Water is metered and can be expensive. If, like many rural dwellers, your water is supplied via its own tank (*cisterna*), you will fill the tank as you require it, from a visiting water truck. You may also have your own well, or borehole (*furo*).

Ask your nearest neighbours, or the vendors/agents of the house to check the availability of water, and how to make contact with the water suppliers. If you live in the countryside and are the proud owners of a swimming pool, be aware that in the event of forest fires (pretty common in the summer, and particularly devastating in 2003), your pool will be sucked dry by emergency helicopters fighting the fire – you have no choice but to let your water go. Often the south endures cuts to supply in the summer due to chronic shortages.

THE POST

The postal services – CTT – are well run in Portugal. Offices usually open from 9am to about 6-ish, longer in bigger towns or tourist areas. Apart from small, rural villages, most towns do have an office. You can also buy stamps at tobacconists' kiosks, and now at a growing number of automatic stamp machines in town squares, airports or stations. The Post Office offers a range of services as you may be used to in the UK; in some you may have to take a numbered ticket as you enter, for your turn, like you do at deli counters in supermarkets. Others may have specific counters (often called *guichets*) for different services. Services you may find:

- *selos*   stamps
- *registrado*   registered post
- *valor declarado*   special registered service
- *encomendas/pacotes*   parcels
- *correio azul*   express, priority mail
- *estrangeiro*   foreign mail

You can also make a phone call from the Post Office. See next section.

If you live in a rural area, where postal deliveries may be rather infrequent, you may decide to have your mail sent to your own box at the Post Office, called an *apartado*. You may either be issued with a key to open your own box, or may have to request mail over the counter. You have to fill in a form to apply for a box, but it is a straightforward process. As usual, you will need ID and proof of address.

COMMUNICATIONS

Funnily enough, you know you can even go to Portugal to live *and* keep in touch with everyone you wish to!

Phones

It is now much easier than it used to be to have a phone installed if your new home does not already have a line. The Portuguese phone company PT (Portugal telecom) has become more efficient, although it is still not cheap to make calls in Portugal. People are now switching to non-PT systems. To request a phone, or have the bill changed to your name, visit the local Telecom office (*Loja da Telecom*), with:

- your *residência*
- ID
- tax number
- proof of address
- bank account details.

Internet
Few households in Portugal have their own computer, but it is perfectly possible to work and use computers there. If you need to keep in touch with people by email and you don't have a computer, there are a few cyber cafes now, some within the PT offices, and other, independent ones, mostly in the Algarve and Lisbon.

Language
Don't forget to keep up your Portuguese-learning once you get out there. Hopefully, you will have made a good start before you left the UK, but keep it going in Portugal:

- read newspapers and magazines
- listen to people
- watch TV
- try a language-swap – some English in exchange for some Portuguese
- many language schools offer courses
- new initiative by the Portuguese government – 'Project of Integration' – free lessons for foreign residents, run by the local parish councils. Check out English press in Portugal, or your local Câmara.

SHOPPING
With the availability of so much fresh produce, the traditional way of shopping for food has always been in

the market-place, and small, specialist shops. Housewives have always bought fresh meat or fish on a daily basis, along with newly-baked bread warm from the bakery, and vegetables and fruit. However, times *are* changing, and whereas previously the local *mercearia* (grocers') and *mini-mercado* (small supermarket) provided a daily supply of produce, a growing number of families now head for one of a number of burgeoning *hipermercados*, and do all their shopping under one roof.

Most of the large chains, such as **Modelo**, **Pão de Açúcar**, **Prisunic**, and **Jumbo**, open late into the evening (and very late at the week-end), the places buzzing with a seemingly never-ending stream of shoppers. Certainly the range of products is impressive – the largest stocking from clothes and books to fresh bread, frozen foods (although only 55% of Portuguese households as yet possess a freezer) and hundreds of lines.

A recent development is the diversification into food retailing of some of the large petrol filling stations. BP, in collaboration with a leading supermarket chain, has been opening up 24-hour *Modelo Expresso* shops at their garages across the country. It seems that much of Portugal is catching up with life in the fast lane, and modifying its shopping habits accordingly.

The range of non-food shops is probably, on the whole, smaller than you are used to in the UK, with only larger towns and cities having any kind of chainstores. Portuguese fashion and shoe shops are plentiful, as the Portuguese are well-dressed people, and these are worth a *visit*. You can also buy bargain items at the monthly feiras, or travelling markets. In the north of Portugal, there are now some factory-outlet stores.

Other shops you may require include:

- *padaria*   baker
- *peixaria*   fishmonger
- *talho*   butcher
- *mercado*   market
- *mercearia*   grocer
- *livraria*   bookshop
- *quiosque/tabacaria*   newsagent/tobacconist
- *farmácia*   chemist
- *loja de moda/boutique*   fashion shop
- *papelaria*   stationer
- *cabeleireiro*   hairdresser
- *oculista*   optician
- *pastelaria*   cake shop/café
- *sapataria*   shoe shop
- *sapateiro*   shoe mender
- *loja de ferragens*   hardware/ironmonger
- *lavandaria*   laundry
- *centro comercial*   shopping centre
- *loja*   shop

In general shop opening times are: Monday to Friday, approximately 9–1 and 3–7. Closed Saturday afternoons. Shopping centres open longer hours, especially at weekends. Markets usually close by mid-afternoon.

According to an Abbey National Offshore Survey what

British expatriates miss most in terms of food are:

- tea bags
- marmite
- baked beans
- fish and chips
- cheddar cheese
- fresh milk
- bacon

and the shops they miss most are:

- Marks and Spencer
- Boots
- corner shop
- newsagent
- Selfridges
- HMV
- Oasis
- Next
- Oddbins

EATING OUT

The Portuguese themselves love eating out. It's part of their social make-up, and it's a pleasant experience, too, for visitors and residents alike. Quite apart from the lunch-time activity, cafés and restaurants fill with couples and families particularly at the week-ends and for Sunday lunch. It is quite usual to see young children out with the family, sometimes until quite late – all are welcome in Portuguese restaurants and Portuguese children behave! Some establishments charge their food according to weight (*comida a peso*), so you help yourself to what you want, and there is a price per kilo. Surprisingly, this works out at a very reasonable deal, as you can fit a lot on a plate before it adds up to very much.

In the Algarve, there is an obvious sop to the tourist trade, with an overwhelming array of English-type eating places, offering English breakfasts, sausage and chips, and burgers-a-plenty. But if you look carefully enough, you'll also find the places the Portuguese frequent, and that is where to go for your more authentic (and cheaper) meals. If you are discerning with your choice and wallet, you can still have a lavish meal with wine for a fraction of the UK price.

Fast-food chains are now drawing custom, particularly at the shopping centres. Youngsters are growing up in the McDonalds era – it now has 100 branches in Portugal. In fact, franchise fast-food outlets, particularly in large shopping centres, are a rapidly-expanding area, and not only for foreign names. '*Mestre Camarão*' (Mister Prawn) is a recent innovation in reasonably-priced sea-food outlets, and other '*restaurantes temáticos*' have been springing up, such as *Cantina Mariachi* (Mexican), *Sumo* (Oriental), and *Skiros* (Greek).

If you want to try some more typical Portuguese meals, look out for:

Costa Verde
Duck (*pato*), octopus, steamed conger-eel, roasted kid (*cabrito assado*), lamprey, a range of smoked hams, tripe (Oporto's famous dish – the people who live there are known as *tripeiros*), dozens of desserts based on the egg-sweets.

Costa de Prata
Many fish dishes, including stews of eel, clams and cockles (*caldeirada*), grilled pork kebabs (*espetadas*), stewed chicken, and kid. Again, many sweet dishes including the *ovos moles* and the bean cakes from Torres Vedras

(*pastéis de feijão*). Dried fruits and preserves.

The Mountain areas

Strong tasting food such as the various sausages, including the *alheiras* (veal and bread) and *morcela* (blood sausage), wholesome stews *(feijoada)*, partridge, trout, and *maranhos* (lamb and chicken giblets cooked with rice). Famous cheeses.

Lisbon area

Lots of fish – bass, mussels, red mullet, swordfish, lobster and crab. Goat and sheep cheeses, special sponge cake (*pão de ló*), Sintra's cheese cakes (*queijadas*), and gin cakes (*zimbros*) from Sesimbra. And don't forget the delicious custard cream pastries – *pastéis de Belém* (or *pastéis de nata*).

The Plains

Stewed eels (*enguias*), lamprey, sausages, kid stew and pork with clams (*carne de porco à alentejana*), hare with red beans and fried rabbit (*coelho*). Tasty bread and cheese, as well as sweet pastries such as the Évora egg and almond paste sweets. Excellent melon, and the famous Elvas sugar plums.

Algarve

Seafood dishes (*mariscos*), including seafood rice and *caldeirada* stew, *cataplana* (copper cooking vessel) dishes, grilled fish, especially sardines. Sweets made from almond and fig paste, often in the shape of fruits and animals.

Madeira and the Azores

Meat and fish kebabs, tuna steaks (*atum*), *peixe-espada*

(scabbard fish) a deep sea fish never seen alive as it dies of decompression before reaching the surface, it is particularly good with banana, octopus stew, yams and pork sausages, honey cake (*bolo de mel*), and tropical fruits and island cheeses.

LOCAL TRANSPORT

Buses and coaches

Buses (*autocarros*) are extremely efficient, serving all parts of towns and cities, cheap, and run on time until they hit rush-hour (*a hora de ponta*). They can become overcrowded, particularly in the larger cities, and with all the Portuguese enjoying a chat – very noisy too. You enter a bus at the front, and usually have to take a ticket from the driver and punch it in a little machine (*obliterador*) just behind him. Doors at the back of the bus let you off. In many places tickets can be bought in multiples, saving money. These '*módulos*' are on sale at little kiosks near the main bus routes.

For travel further afield, services around the country have improved in recent years, and now you can get a coach (*camioneta*) to most parts of Portugal, at a very cheap fare. The older coaches, from companies such as EVA, and *Rede Expressos* in the north, are a more basic style and tend to get over-hot in the summer. Increasingly, however, investment is being made in new, state-of-the-art luxury coaches, with air-conditioning, and some with hostess-service for drinks and snacks.

Trains (*Comboios*)

The railway network, **Caminhos de Ferro Portugueses**

(CP), is a state-owned company, running a system of approximately 3,000 km of track. Trains are very reliable, cheap, and a great way to see Portugal; unfortunately the network does not reach very far through inland areas. A modernisation plan is currently underway for the whole network, and there are already new high-speed (Alfa) trains linking Lisbon and Oporto (314 km) in around 3 hours. Plans are afoot to link the Lisbon–Madrid route on to Barcelona and Paris, with the acclaimed AVE/TGV trains. 2003 saw the inauguration of the new railway connection from Faro to Lisbon via the new Vasco de Gama bridge. At the moment there is only one train a day running, with a journey time of approximately 4 hours 20. Seats must be reserved in advance.

The ordinary trains are huge, silver machines, whose steps are very difficult to climb up. Inside the carriages, the bench-seats are comfortable, and high up so you have a great view, but you will often share your journey with a number of locals, who will nod and smile at you, so it's a good opportunity to talk to people. Children under 4 travel free on public transport, and there are good discounts for those aged 4–12, students and anyone over 65.

TRANSPORT IN LISBON

All transport in the capital, apart from the Metro, is run by the state-owned company **Carris**. Their kiosks are seen all over the city, selling tickets and a variety of travel cards for the different zones of travel, or 4 and 7-day tourist passes. Lisbon also now offers a special 'Lisbon Card', with access to all public transport, and free entry to some museums and monuments. One of the novelties of getting about are the trams (*os eléctricos*), built originally in Sheffield, Britain, pre-World War I. The older ones trundle through the streets of down-town (*a Baixa*) and up the hills at either side, to the districts (*os bairros*) beyond. More modern styles have been introduced, with two carriages joined together with flexible rubber so they bend round corners, and a mechanised voice informing you of each stop.

The underground (*o metropolitano*)

The metro is a small, but expanding system in Lisbon, whose entrances are marked above ground by a large red M. The original system had just three arms to it, but was extended in preparation for Expo 98. The 'Oriente' station, at the Expo site, is an example of beautiful modern architecture, with expanses of tiled surroundings. Stops hitherto unreachable under the ground have now opened up, with a system that is swift and efficient, albeit uncomfortably crowded at peak times. Information and maps are available at Metro stations and the Turismo offices.

WHERE TO FIND HELP

For practical advice on aspects of life in Portugal, you can:

- contact your local Town Hall (*Câmara*)

- check the English publications

- definitely join AFPOP – even before setting off for Portugal

- ask the Portuguese Consulate in the UK for information

- when in Portugal, use free phone 800-296-296 for information (including in English) on travel, hospitals, police, tourism

- check out *www.dgturismo.pt* and *www.icep.pt*

- talk to people whilst you are there – make contacts and build up reference material.

For real newcomers to Portugal, the *Collins Portuguese Language Survival Guide* is a very useful book, full of pictures of everyday signs, items, tickets, instructions to use, timetables, food and drink. It is also available with a CD to practise some basic phrases.

(14)

Enjoying Life in Portugal

Now that you're settling in, and you're managing the routine aspects of life, it's time to enjoy yourself – after all, you've probably earned it by now, and people are doing it all around you. Now, I don't know what kind of social life you may have been used to in the UK, or what hobbies you may have pursued in your free time, but it is probably fair to say that some of your leisure pursuits may take on a new angle in Portugal.

There may not be access to the sorts of activities you have previously enjoyed, or you may not be able to buy some of the items connected with your pastimes. But that is not to say that you can't have fun – it may just require a bit of re-thinking. Of course, in the Algarve, there is a ready-made network of ex-patriot activities too, so you'll have to decide which way to take your pursuit of pleasure. What follows is an overview of the sorts of activities you might consider – location will render some of them easier to follow than others. The Directory on page 235 lists some details of places to contact for further information.

LEISURE FACILITIES

Whilst Portugal does not have the same network of leisure and sports centres, as in the UK, often run by Town Councils, the Portuguese do enjoy sports, mostly out-doors, and many connected with water – and with a coastline of 800km, that is not really surprising.

There are many Municipal swimming baths around the country, some indoors, but many outside. My husband and I went to a pool up in the higher Douro town of Moncorvo, on a hot and dusty August afternoon, and found practically all of the inhabitants of the town there too – the ideal way to keep cool, and with a pool set high on a hill with wild countryside around, it was truly a fantastic setting for a dip – and extremely cheap too. We paid about 80 pence each. You are usually requested to wear a bathing cap (*touca*), and if you don't have one, you will be asked to buy one there, for about a pound.

In the Algarve, and some areas around Lisbon in particular, there are now a number of gyms, many private (and in the south usually belonging to the larger hotels). On holiday you can normally have access to the facilities at your hotel or complex, and as a resident you can become a member just as you might in the UK.

The Portuguese love the beach as much as the next person, and when they are on holiday, or have free time with their families, that is where they will often head. In the Algarve, you are spoiled for sandy stretches, with amazing rocky cliffs and outcrops. The water is generally quite clean and safe, although it is not always that warm – it is still predominantly Atlantic. The Atlantic coastline itself, from north to south, is one wondrous beach after another, from the silvery delights of places like **Vila Praia d'Âncora**, right down through Lisbon's **Costa da Caparica**, and the wild coasts of the lower **Alentejo** through to **Sagres** in the south. Crashing waves, cold-ish water, even in summer, but certainly, *the* place to be, with beach tents, picnics and games.

Other popular pursuits include:

- **Surfing/windsurfing** (*surf/wind-surf*)
  Very popular with youngsters, and Portugal is highly ranked in International competitions. Good places for the surf include the beaches along from Lisbon – Guincho and Praia das Maçãs.

- **Sailing** (*vela*)
  Numerous marinas and clubs, mostly the domain of foreign visitors. Vilamoura in the Algarve is the best-known, top-class marina.

- **Diving** (*mergulho*)
  Some diving offered, mostly in the Algarve.

- **Cycling** (*ciclismo*)
  Although the Portuguese themselves rarely cycle, they

do enjoy it as a sport. There are annual Tours of Portugal, mountain races, BMX competitions, and the *Volta ao Algarve* (Tour of the Algarve). Bikes can be hired in some resorts in the Algarve, but you need to be cautious on the roads.

◆ **Horse riding (*hipismo*)**
see: *www.equus.algarve.com*
Although growing in popularity, still the domain of the more affluent. Some trekking and a growing number of riding centres in the Algarve, Lisbon. No horse races for betting on.

◆ **Hunting and fishing (*caça/pesca*)**
Shooting in rural areas very popular/fishing very common – both sea and fresh-water. Licences are cheap. Fishing trips are plentiful in the Algarve, setting out from many resorts. You can also go on trips to spot dolphins, or just to have a great visit to some of the rocky crags.

◆ **Football (*futebol/a bola*)**
The nation's favourite spectator sport, and one played by most youngsters on any bit of ground they can find. TV games are avidly followed in bars and cafes, or on transistor radios as men (still by far the predominant fan) stroll along in parks or promenades. The most well-known teams are Benfica and Sporting (both Lisbon), and Porto FC. 2004 sees Portugal as host to the Euro competition, and in preparation, 5 new stadia have been built and 5 renovated around the country (and we still haven't got a new Wembley...?).

◆ **Tennis, basketball, volleyball, handball, roller skating, hockey (*ténis, basquetebol, voleibol, andebol, patinagem em linha, hóquei*)**
Best facilities for tennis in the Algarve, at some of the private fitness clubs or exclusive resorts; other sports are on a smaller scale, but available in some areas.

◆ **Bull fighting (*corrida de touros/tourada*)**
Not as fanatical as their Spanish counterparts, but still fairly popular. Fighting on horseback, plus other displays. Large ring in Lagos.

GOLF

Golf is undoubtedly a pulling-factor for many Brits buying in the Algarve. As a top-flight world destination for golf, Portugal boasts many world-class courses, with 11 of the Algarve's in the World top 100 list. The Algarve is often voted a major international destination for the sport, and its facilities are second to none. Surprisingly, there are no famous Portuguese golf stars, but there are certainly thousands of would-be foreign ones. Some of the plushest resorts in the Algarve are built around courses, such as **Parque da Floresta**. Some of the best courses include **Vale do Lobo**, **Quinta do Lago**, **Vilamoura** and **Penina**. The *Algarve Golf Guide* magazine is a useful source of information, and bargain rounds can be found via the following websites:

www.tee-times.info
www.algarvegolf.net
www.algarvegolfdesk.net
www.algarvebookings.com

THE ARTS

Lisbon and Oporto are blessed with a number of high-standard venues for taking in theatre, opera, other musical events, including *Fado* evenings, and many galleries, museums and places of artistic interest. Most cities and towns of a certain size also have places where cultural interests can be pursued. Portugal has a long heritage of art, crafts, music and literature, and the Portuguese are keen to promote that side of their country. Music, in particular, is popular across the ages, with a range from traditional *Fado* and folklore music, to modern pop and rock, jazz and acclaimed classical artists such as the pianist Artur Pizarro. In smaller places, the village may well have its own band, which plays at community dances (*bailes*), where everyone comes out and has a good night out together. Festivals are a common link throughout Portugal. There are national feast days, but also each town or village may have its own festivities of some kind throughout the year. The cinema is also a popular venue for entertainment; many towns have one, and it's pretty cheap.

INDOOR HOBBIES

It is not as common for the Portuguese to indulge in hobbies such as collecting things, model-making, or to go to evening classes for leisure purposes. You will find some of the International schools may run a handful of that type of class for adults, but it is not widespread. If you have a hobby you would like to carry on whilst in Portugal, it is worthwhile asking your local UK supplier of materials (if relevant) if you can order stuff from them whilst abroad. You may not necessarily find what you are looking for in Portugal. Indoors, the Portuguese mostly just watch TV, and to an alarming level, according to recent Portuguese surveys. As few homes have their own computers, that is not as advanced a form of home entertainment as in the UK, and even reading loses out to the Big Box, where there are now four TV channels, plus access to satellite, especially in the Algarve.

SOCIALISING WITH OTHER FOREIGNERS

Whether you feel you need a prop to start with, in the body of people who speak your own language, or if you want to make ex-patriots the focus of your life anyway, there are plenty of things to do in the ex-pat cradle, especially in the Algarve, and to a smaller extent around Lisbon and Oporto, where the other main foreign communities are found. A lot of socialising centres around drinks and eating out, and why not, given the good food and cheap prices? There are other things, too. A glance down the To Do section of the English newspapers and magazines will throw up:

- line dancing
- car boot sales
- charity events
- charity golf events
- golf tournaments
- theatrics
- tennis tournaments
- bridge
- openings of restaurants, galleries, art exhibitions
- bowls
- walking and running clubs.

There are also a number of established British societies and clubs, such as the Royal British Legion, St Andrew's Society, the WRVS. Others are included on: *www.bcclisbon.org*

Holiday villages and complexes often have their own entertainment too, such as musical events and food evenings.

Whilst it is always comforting to be surrounded by at least familiar language when in unknown territory, it can be a shame to miss out on getting to know your Portuguese neighbours and, dare I say it, hosts!

MAKING PORTUGUESE FRIENDS

So, where can you go to make some Portuguese friends? You can start with the people living near you (unless you are on an all-foreign enclave of a complex). If you have taken on board what I said about learning some of the language, you can try some friendly everyday phrases, which will at least endear you more than Mr X, who has lived in the Algarve for 23 years and still can't even say 'Good morning' properly (or perhaps doesn't want to be bothered). Once you make a start on dialogue, the Portuguese will open up immensely to you, and it won't be long before you are invited in for coffee, or to see their house (they are all fiercely proud of their homes, however humble they may be).

Other places you will find Portuguese hovering are:

♦ in bars and cafés, especially when there is football on the TV

- working in your hotel/resort/complex/villa
- shops, markets and in the street
- football matches
- the beach, swimming pools
- on buses and trains
- night-clubs
- parties and festivals
- family gatherings, such as baptisms and first communions, weddings, birthdays – if you are lucky to be invited, it's a great occasion to make some friends.

My very good friend Peter Norris, who is a frequent visitor to Portugal, never misses the opportunity to pass the time of day with Portuguese people. As he did bother to learn the language to quite a good level, he is happy to have a go, and will always have a chat with people in bars and cafés, or whilst he is travelling. The encounters he has, and stories he can recount are testimony to what happens when you make the effort.

RELIGION, CUSTOMS AND ETIQUETTE

Portugal is a predominantly Catholic country, with 97% of the population professing to that faith. However, the power of the church and its appeal to the masses has certainly diminished in recent years. The north has always been the stronghold of the church, and it is here today it is still a uniting force, albeit weaker now than at any other time in its history. The south has never had the same alliance with the church, although there are still religious festivals and people do attend church. Most people, as in many countries, now attend at special times such as weddings, Christmas and Easter, but not much else.

Other religions are represented on a much smaller scale: there are Jewish and Muslim communities, mainly in and around Lisbon and the Alentejo, and Lisbon also has the only church of the Christian Scientist Movement.

In the ex-patriot communities there are also the following churches, often meeting in small halls or hotel rooms:

◆ Church of England
◆ Church of Scotland
◆ British-run RC church
◆ Salvation Army
◆ Anglican
◆ International Christian Fellowship
◆ Evangelical
◆ 7th Day Adventist
◆ Jehovah's Witnesses
◆ Baptist
◆ Jewish.

Find details of meetings in the *Algarve Resident* or *The News/APN*.

As befits a predominantly Catholic country, many celebrations are connected with the Church Calendar year, but as a people so tied to the rural and coastal way of life, they also celebrate festivals of the land and sea. In particular religion and lifestyle come together, as in the blessing of fishing boats, but at other times festivals are more firmly steeped in Celtic and pagan customs. There are 13 official public holidays in Portugal, when the whole nation joins in both religious and secular celebrations of

Holy Days and commemorations of important historical dates. Additionally, though, every region has its own calendar of local festivals and events, translating into a national list of hundreds, if not thousands of local festivities.

PUBLIC HOLIDAYS IN PORTUGAL

New Year	*Ano Novo*	1 January
Carnival	*Carnaval*	February/March
Easter	*Páscoa*	April
Liberty Day	*Dia da Liberdade*	25 April
Labour Day	*Dia do Trabalhador*	1 May
Corpus Christi	*Corpo de Deus*	June
Portugal Day	*O Dia de Portugal*	10 June
St. Anthony's Day	*Santo António*	13 June (Lisbon)
St. John's Day	*São João*	24 June (Oporto)
Assumption Day	*Assunção de Nossa Senhora*	15 August
Republic Day	*Implantação da República*	5 October
All Saints Day	*Dia de Todos os Santos*	1 November
Restoration of Independence Day	*Restauração da Independência*	1 December
Immaculate Conception	*Imaculada Conceição*	8 December
Christmas	*Natal*	25 December

ETIQUETTE

The Portuguese are a very courteous people, whose way of life is steeped in layers of polite behaviour and forms of address. When talking with someone you do not know, or with older people, you should address them as '*o senhor*' (men) and '*a senhora*' (ladies). People with university degrees are usually called *doutor/doutora*, and those with professions such as engineering, architecture, teaching, also take titles such as: *o senhor engenheiro*, or *a senhora professora*.

Keeping appointments is important, especially in a business context, although infuriatingly, the Portuguese may keep you waiting ages before turning up themselves. Meetings can go on a long time, often over meals and drinks. On a social level, punctuality is not a great art of the Portuguese, so allow extra if you are planning to meet anywhere.

Dress is important. The Portuguese are always well-presented, wearing suits to work, and smart outfits to go out. If you are invited to their homes, it is customary to take a small gift, such as flowers or chocolates, and take an interest as they proudly show you their house and possessions.

PLACES OF INTEREST

In Chapter 2 I listed some of the great things to see and do in the various regions of Portugal. There is no shortage of pleasant trips and days out, wherever you make your home there. Guide books give you much more information, and many more ideas; friends and family will give you more. Build up your own memories as you go along. Here are just some of what I would put on a wish-list of what not to miss whilst in Portugal:

The North
- ◆ Peneda Gerês National Park
- ◆ Douro valley by train, up to Vila Real and Mateus Palace

- Oporto wine cellars
- Ponte de Lima
- Barcelos and its cockerels
- rugged landscapes of Trás-os-Montes

Centre
- Coimbra and Portugal dos Pequeninos (Portugal in miniature)
- Aveiro lagoon
- Serra da Estrela mountains
- Conímbriga Roman ruins
- Seaside resorts such as Figueira da Foz
- Buçaco forest

Lisbon and Tejo valley
- All of Lisbon, especially Alfama, castle, Bairro Alto nightlife, Eduardo VII park, custard cakes in Belém
- Sintra
- Train to Cascais and Estoril
- Costa da Caparica beaches
- Arrábida coast and hills
- Tagus and Sado bird estuaries
- Alcobaça and Batalha church buildings

The Plains
- Évora and chapel of bones
- Elvas aqueduct and walled town with views across to Spain
- Estremoz marble quarries
- Monsaraz walled town
- Atlantic coastline

Algarve
- Silves Moorish castle
- Ria Formosa bird reserve
- Wild coast to the West
- Monchique hills and Spa
- Cabo de São Vicente
- Lagos old quarters and slave market

SUMMARY

You have no excuse for not knowing what to do with your free time in Portugal. There is plenty to occupy you, whether you choose to be inside or without the ex-patriot communities. It may not all be exactly the sort of leisure routines you may have grown accustomed to in the UK, but other things will take their place. For those willing to go out and look for it, there really is something for all ages and tastes in Portugal.

Changing Your Mind

Sadly, things may not work out the way you intended, and for a variety of reasons, both concrete and psychological, you may end up having to admit it is time to move on, and move back. Some situations can be avoided by careful planning and circumspect management, others are simply thrown in the way and depending on your circumstances, you'll either sink or swim by them.

REASONS FOR CHANGE

Although there are some definite long-stay residents in the Algarve, and a handful elsewhere in Portugal, and the vast majority of mid-term visitors come back year-on-year, there are also those who, for one reason or another, just do not hack it, and decide, or are obliged to move back 'home'. These reasons may include:

- lack of work
- lack of what is deemed 'suitable' work
- lack of work for partner
- non-integration into Portuguese life
- not at ease with foreign community/too 'British'/ 'Dutch'/'German' etc.
- boredom – too much non-routine leisure time
- run out of money
- illness
- bereavement – either in Portugal or back in UK
- business goes bust
- legal problems
- family squabbles
- good old-fashioned homesickness.

Now you may be saying 'well that won't happen to me, as I'm not one of those all-day G&T drinkers, I'm a grafter, I'm not running away from anything/anyone in the UK, my nose is clean etc etc'. That may well be true, but with the best will in the world, the unexpected does happen when you are abroad, and learning to cope with eventualities is part of the process of having a happy and continued life out there.

AVOIDING FAILURE

So, how can you minimalise the types of problems which may send you scuttling back to Old Blighty?

- Be realistic about your expectations, how long it will take to settle in, what you will be able to achieve, and what life there will be like.

- Prepare beforehand by learning about the place, the people and how they tick.

- Learn Portuguese!

- Think about the kind of work you *could* do, not what you *can* do.

- Be prepared to go out and look for work.

- Be flexible in what you will accept – work/wages/ conditions.

- Think about how your family will cope – what can your partner do?

- Be strong as a family unit and plan things together.

- Try not to succumb to the cheap drink – keep it in moderation.

- Keep fit and healthy so you can avoid unnecessary illnesses.

- Keep in touch with people back home, and try to arrange visits from them.

- Be nice to yourself and treat yourself sometimes, even a good long walk on a summery morning can work wonders for low morale.

- Be prepared professionally, if you are taking up work for a company out there.

- Try to establish a network of colleagues or acquaintances who will be there in times of need.

- Budget ahead for all eventualities – do not under-estimate how much you may need to tide you over.

- Above all, keep a sense of humour!

If all else fails, remember, at least you chose Portugal, and not New Zealand – it will only take you around 3 hours to get home!

SELLING UP

So, it's time to let it go, that dream home in the sun. Never mind, you can start again, it's been an experience, and hopefully with positive points to take with you. One compensation is that, even within a short time out there, your property may well have increased in price, so you may be able to make something out of it. You do have the option of keeping it (if you are financially able to) and renting it out. In that way, you'll have a steady income from it, and still be able to use it as a holiday home yourself when you feel ready to again. Otherwise, if it's to be the definitive move away, you'll need to sell the property, either using the same channels as you did when you bought – estate agent and legal representation – or by a combination of advertising through papers, magazines, through family and friends, internet, plus a good lawyer.

From the point of view of the legal and financial aspects of selling, the process would be:

- Make sure you have a good agent and a solicitor.

- You need all the documentation relating to the property.

- Once the promissory contract is signed, if you back out, you will have to pay the purchaser twice the original deposit.

- You will need to visit the tax department to see what capital gains and tax will be owing.

- The *Escritura* (deed of transfer) is signed.

- Consider how you wish any excess profit to be paid – either into a euro account, or immediately transferred back to sterling – it is worth keeping an eye on the currency market before you make an instant decision.

Provided you have sought guidance from professionals, and have good advice in the form of an English-speaking lawyer, there is no reason to think that selling will be any more difficult than buying.

...AND MOVING OUT

If you have just rented a place, you may not have many big items or belongings to move back to the UK. You may be able to do the move in a couple of car journeys, or leave some stuff with friends for subsequent visits. Don't forget, if you are in rented accommodation, to check what kind of notice you are legally bound to give of your intended departure, and let the landlord know in writing.

If you have more substantial items to move back, you would be wise to do it through one of the many experienced removals firms with bases in Portugal. You may already have used one for your move there in the first place. There is no shortage. See Directory for some suggestions, or contact the British Association of

Removers, Tel: 020-8861-3331 for a list of their members who specifically deal with Portugal.

SUMMARY

The reason behind your move may have been totally out of your hands, in which case you'll need to be philosophical and try to get on with what has come your way. It may not necessarily mean the end to your dream of a home in Portugal; it may simply be a blip in proceedings, and you may get another chance, in which case you'll have all the accrued knowledge and experience so that it will be far easier next time anyway.

If your situation was something which could have been avoided, then it must serve as a learning curve, and hopefully it will not have been such an expensive one as to deny you the opportunity to try again sometime. Better luck next time!

Directory of Useful Information

For ease of reference, the directory is divided into sections relating to topics covered in the book. Details were correct at time of writing, however no guarantee can be given that information has not changed in the meantime: websites in particular are subject to change. The author is always grateful for updates on information, plus feedback or recommendations for inclusion in further editions. Please write c/o the publishers.

The following publications are also a wealthy source of contacts and useful information:

Buying property in Portugal information pack, Portuguese-UK Chamber of Commerce, 4th floor, 22/25a Sackville Street, London W1X 1DE. Tel: 020-7494 1844. Fax: 020-7494 1822

AFPOP Directory of services to members, plus *Insight* magazines: AFPOP, Apartado 728, 8501-917 Portimão, Algarve. Tel: 282-458 509. Fax: 282-458 277. Email: *afpop@mail.telepac.pt*

Welcome to Porto, Oporto Mothers' Group, Rua Luís de Camões 263, Miramar, 4405-088 Arcozelo VNG. Tel/fax: 753-1843

Feeling at home in Portugal, International Women in Portugal Organisation, Apartado 1060, 2750 Cascais, Lisbon

PORTUGAL/GENERAL INTEREST

Contacts

Portuguese Embassy, 11 Belgrave Square, London SW1Z 8PP. Tel: 020-7235 5331

Anglo-Portuguese Society, Canning House, 2 Belgrave Square, London SW1X 8PJ. Tel: 020-7245 9738

ICEP Portuguese Trade and Tourism Office – see address above for Chamber of Commerce

Websites

ICEP – Portuguese Trade and Tourism Organisation, *www.portugal-insite.pt*

Instituto Meteorologia – the weather, *www.meteo.pt*

Portugal-info – information for travellers, especially from USA, *www.portugal-info.net*

Oporto Town Hall – local information, *www.cm-porto.pt*

Lisbon Town Hall – local information, *www.cm-lisboa.pt*

Algarve information, *www.algarve.com*

List of Portuguese sites, *www.portembassy.gla.uk/portpages.html*

Portugal Virtual – lots of links, has an English version, *www.portugalvirtual.pt*

Portugal na Rede – general, cultural and commercial links, *www.interacesso.pt/lugares/portnet/htm*

Countrywatch site on Portugal – very useful on all aspects.

Páginas Portuguesas: *www.Paginas-Portuguesas.com*

www.lonelyplanet.com

AFPOP site: *www.afpop.com*

Portuguese search engines

SAPO, *www.sapo.pt*

TERRA VISTA, *www.terravista.pt*
PORTUGALNET, *www.portugalnet.pt*
BUSCANET, *www.busca.net*
PORTUGALWEB, *www.portugalweb.pt*
PORTAL DE PORTUGAL, www.portal.pt

Reading/resources

The Portuguese: The Land and its People, Marion Kaplan (Penguin, 2nd rev. edn 1998)

Portugal: A Companion History, J H Saraiva (Carcanet, 1997)

Prince Henry 'The Navigator' – A Life, Peter Russell (Yale University Press, 1999)

A New History of Portugal, H V Livermore (Cambridge University Press, 1976, 2nd edn)

The Portuguese Seaborne Empire 1415–1825, C R Boxer (Carcanet, 1973)

Portugal's Struggle for Liberty, Mário Soares (Allen and Unwin, 1975)

Off the Beaten Track – Portugal, Nick Timmons (MPC, 1992)

Insight Guides Portugal, Alison F. Hill (ed.) (APA, 1989)

Eyewitness Guides – Portugal with Madeira and the Azores, (Dorling Kindersley, 1997)

Backwards out of the Big World: A Voyage into Portugal, Paul Hyland (Flamingo paperback, 1998)

A Small Death in Lisbon, crime novel by Robert Wilson (Harper Collins, 2000) gives good background to the Salazar regime, including relationships with Britain and Germany during the War, and police investigations

The Company of Strangers, Robert Wilson (HarperCollins, 2002)

Portugal: 50 Years of Dictatorship, António de Figueiredo (Penguin, 1975)

Insight on Portugal: The Year of the Captains, Sunday Times (André Deutsch, 1975)

Portugal Matters – Education Matters, 29 High Street, Halberton, Tiverton, Devon EX16 7AF. Tel: 01884-820081

Vida Nova (magazine for the Portuguese in the UK), 106 Victoria Road, London NW6 6QB. Tel: 020-7625 5672. Fax: 020-7461 0387

Páginas Portuguesas (telephone directory of Portuguese services/contacts in UK), J R Publications, 48 Norfolk Avenue, South Tottenham, London N15 6JX. Tel: 020-88007628. Fax: 020-8800 0050. Email: *paginas.portuguesas@btinternet.com*

FINDING PROPERTY
Contacts

Cambridge Trading International Ltd, 83-85 Dunstable Street, Ampthill, Bedford MK45 2NQ. Tel: 01525-405900

Property Search Portugal, The Gables, Bell Lane, Cassington, Witney, Oxon. OX8 1DS. Tel: 01865-883154. Fax: 01865-883301

Cerro Novo Lda, The Manor House, Edington, Westbury, Wiltshire BA13 4QW. Tel: 01380-831411. Fax: 01380-831455

Mike Hough Associates (Agricultural), The Laurels, Mill Road, Bintree, Dereham, Norfolk NR20 5NL. Tel: 01362-683790. Fax: 01362-684175

Pugh Homes, 42 Walcott Avenue, Christchurch, Dorset

BH23 2NG. Tel/fax: 01202-487396

IDANA Algarve Imobiliária Lda, Rua João de Deus 43, 8250 São Brás de Alportel, Algarve. Tel: 289-842369

IN's, Av. Eng. Duarte Pacheco, Torre 2-5, Sala 9, Amoreiras, 1070 Lisboa. Tel: 383-2777

Fernandes e Costa Lda (represented by Bailey & Ambler, Grantham), Av. Almirante Reis 104-2, 1100 Lisboa. Tel: 812-3231

Predial Zela Lda, Rua António Maria Cardoso 15-1, 1200 Lisboa. Tel: 347-5448

Movi, Agência Imobiliária Lda (represented by Palmer & Parker), Av.Marginal 9348, 1 Esq., 2750 Cascais. Tel: 483-1032

Algarve Property Group (various offices). Tel: 289-312 383. Email: *info@algarvepropertygroup.com*

Marcela Propriedades, Rua 25 de Abril 31. Tel: 282-768 428/ Fax: 282-762 741. Email: *antonio.marcela@mail.-telepac.pt* Also in Luz

Websites

Algarve Resident: *www.rapicom.com/resident*
www.europropertysearch.com
www.holidayhome.co.uk
www.algarvepropertygroup.com
www.algarve-realestate.com/marcela

Reading/resources

Anglo-Portuguese News (APN), Rua Melo e Sousa 33A, 2765 Estoril. Tel: 466-1471. Fax: 466-0358

Algarve Resident, Rua 16 de Janeiro 6, 8400 Lagoa. Tel: 282-342936. Fax: 282-342939.
Email: *algarveresident@mail.telepac.pt*

HOTELS AND RENTALS
Contacts

Youth Hostels Association, 14 Southampton Street, London WC2.

ENATUR (Pousadas), Av. Santa Joana Princesa 10A, 1700 Lisboa. Tel: 21-844 2001

Assoc. Portuguesa de Pousadas de Juventude (Youth Hostels), Movijovem, Av. Duque D'Ávila 137, 1050 Lisboa. Tel: 21-3559081. Fax: 21-3528621

Websites

Pousadas: *www.pousadas.pt*

Camping: *www.roteiro-campista.pt*

LEGAL SERVICES
Contacts

Figuereido e Co, Berkeley House, 3rd floor, 73 Upper Richmond Road, London SW15, 2SZ. Tel: 020-8877 3844. Fax: 020-8877 0556

Lita Gale Solicitors, 43-45 Gower Street, London WC1E 6HH. Tel: 020-7580 2066. Fax: 020-7580 2067

Neville de Rougemont e Associados, City Cloisters, Suite C4, 188-196 Old Street, London EC1V 8BP. Tel: 020-7490 4656 (also in Lagos and Lisbon)

Noronha Advogados, Suite 1, 52 Ennismore Gardens, London SW7 1AH. Tel: 020-7581 5040

William Oddy Sampson e Co, Praça da República 12-3 Esq., 8800 Tavira, Algarve (also in Lagoa and Almancil)

Mr R P Duarte, Rua João Grave 125, 1FTR. 16, 4100 Porto

International Legal Cooperation, Av. Comunidade Lusíada, Edifício Casa dos Arcos, Loja 7, 8500-801

Portimão. Tel: 282-412 988. Fax: 282-412 998. Email: *reineke-coll@clix.pt*

Soares e Giering Lawyers, Rua Dr Afonso Costa, 4A-1 Esq, 8400-317 Lagoa. Tel: 282-353 274. Fax: 282-353 907. Email: *Sofia-Soares@clix.pt*

J.Plácido Santos e Associados Law Firm, Largo 5 de Outubro 9-10, 1, Apt. 186, 8401-903 Lagoa. Tel: 282-340 250. Fax: 282-342 928. Email: *jpslaw@clix.pt* Also in Almancil

Marante, Almeida, Ferreia Associados Law Office, Rua do Índico, Edifício Altis 3, Q.Cerro Alagoa, 8200-139 Albufeira. Tel: 289-586 888. Fax: 289-586 431. Email: *amealex@mail.telepac.pt* Also in Lagoa and Quinta do Lago

FINANCIAL SERVICES
Contacts

Allan Wright (Canada Life Assurance Co), Albany House, Dollis Mews, Dollis Park, Finchley, London N3 1HH. Tel: 020-8346 2651

Blackstone Franks, Barbican House, 26-34 Old Street, London EC1V 9HL. Tel: 020-7250 3300

Bone e Co Insurance Brokers, 69A Castle Street, Farnham, Surrey GU9 7LP. Tel: 01252-724140

Brown Shipley Lomond Ltd, 84 Coombe Road, New Malden, Surrey KT3 4QS. Tel: 020-8949 8811

Dave Tester Expatriate Insurance Services, 18A Hove Park Villas, Hove BN3 6HG. Tel: 01273-703469. Fax: 01273-777723. Email: *dave.tester@compuserve.com*

Expat Tax Consultants, Churchfield House, North Drive, Hebburn, Tyne and Wear NE31 1ES. Tel: 0191-483 7805

Expatriate Advisory Services, 14 Gordon Road, West Bridgeford, Nottingham NG2 5LN. Tel: 01602-816572

Expats International, 29 Lacon Road, London SE22 9HE. Tel: 020-8229 2484

Hall-Godwins Overseas, Briarcliff House, Kingsmead, Farnborough, Hants GU14 7TE. Tel: 01252-521701

Ronald M Collins and Co, Chartered Accountants, Downs Court Business Centre, 29 The Downs, Altrincham, Cheshire WA14 2QD. Tel: 0161-941 2868

Seatax Ltd (tax advisers), 100 East Iaith Gate, Doncaster DN1 1JA. Tel: 01302-364673

Wilfred T. Fry Ltd, Crescent House, Crescent Road, Worthing BN11 1RN. Tel: 01903-231545. Fax: 01903-200868

David Hills Insurance Agency, Rua Vasco da Gama No. 259, 8135-149 Almancil. Tel: 289-399 774. Fax: 289-397 215 Email: *d.hills.insure.@mail.telepac.pt*

Medal Insurance Brokers Lda, Rua Teófilo Braga 3A 1A/B, Apt. 948, 8501-919 Portimão. Tel: 282-430 800. Fax: 282-430 809. Email: *info@medal.pt*

Sovereign Group (offshore services), Lagoa. Tel: 282-340480. Fax: 282-342259.
Email: *port@SovereignGroup.com*

Banks

Barclays Bank Plc, International Banking Group, 168 Fenchurch Street, London EC3P 3HP. Tel: 020-7283 8989

Banco Espírito Santo e Comercial de Lisboa, 33 Queen Street, London EC4R 1ES. Tel: 020-7332 4300. Fax: 020-7332 4340

Banco Pinto e Sotto Mayor, 5th floor, 10 Philpot Lane, London EC3M 8AA. Tel: 020-7626 5021

Banco de Portugal, Rua do Comércio 148, 1100 Lisboa. Tel: 21-346 2931

Abbey National Offshore, Ed. Cor de Rosa, EN125, Quatro Estradas, 8125-024 Quarteira. Tel: 289-397 900. Fax: 289-397 889.
Email: *portugal@anoffshore.com*

Accountancy firms

Arthur Andersen and Co, 1 Surrey Street, London WC2R 2PS. Tel: 020-7438 3000

Ernst and Young, Rolls House, 7 Rolls Buildings, Fetter Lane, London EC4A 1NH. Tel: 020-7831 7130

KPMG Peat Marwick, 1 Puddle Dock, Blackfriars, London EC4V 3PD. Tel: 020-7236 8000

Price Waterhouse, Av. da Liberdade, 245-7B, 1250 Lisboa. Tel: 21-311 3300

Ernst and Young, Rua Gonçalo Sampaio, 271-4 Esq., 4150 Porto. Tel: 22-600 2015

Deloitte Ross Tohmatsu, Empreendimento das Amoreiras, Av. Eng. Duarte Pacheco, Torre 1, 12 andar, 1000 Lisboa.

Websites

Insurance: *www.medal.pt*
Insurance: *www.davidhills.com*

Reading/resources

A Guide to the Portuguese Property Tax Reforms, Rosemary de Rougemont, Tel: 01628-778566.
Email: *ndr@nevillederougemont.com*

TIMESHARE INFORMATION
Contacts

RCI Europe Ltd, Clarendon House, Station Road, Kettering, Northants NN15 7QT. Tel: 01536-310101

Websites

www.rci.co.uk

www.keyworldinvest.com

www.guidetotimeshare.com

BUILDING, RENOVATING AND DEVELOPERS
Contacts

Importeco Kitchen Specialists, Complexo Industrial do Carmo, EN125, Lagoa. Tel: 282-343 645/6. Fax: 282-343 124

Domus Heating, Importer e Distributor, EN125, Sitio Benfarras, 8100 Boliqueime. Tel: 289-322 852. Fax: 289-322 894

Brooks Kitchens, Rua José Ventura Neto, Cabrita, Lt.3, Loja B, Lagos. Tel: 282-798 966. Fax: 282-799 655

Aguaconcept Lda (water systems), Apt. 279, Silves. Tel: 282-441 313. Fax: 282-441 314

Joro (home systems/equipment), Rua 5 de Outubro, 200, 8135-103 Almancil. Tel: 289-390 830. Fax: 289-390 839. Email: *joro@clix.pt* Also in Lisbon: Tel: 214-569 026/7

Tim Bebbington Quality Paints, Espiche. Tel/fax: 282-789 812

HOME/CIN paints, Parque Empresarial do Algarve, Lote 12 r/c, 8400 Lagoa. Tel: 282-342 795. Fax: 282-341 767. Also in Portimão

Centro de Lareiras (Fireplace Centre), EN125, Vale de Lousas, 8365-027 Alcantarilha. Tel: 282-314 188. Fax:

282-322 670. Email: *centro.lareiras@mail.telepac.pt*
SACL, Serviços de Ar Condicionado Lda (heating/cooling systems), Vale de Lousas, EN125, 8365-027 Alcantarilha. Tel: 282-314 190. Fax: 282-314 191. Email: *sacl@mail.telepac.pt*

LANGUAGE AND CULTURE
Contacts
Association of Translation Companies, Alexandra House, Alexandra Terrace, Guildford GU1 3DA. Tel: 01483-456486

Association for Language Learning, 150 Railway Terrace, Rugby CV21 3HN. Tel: 01788-546443. Fax: 01788-544149. Email: *langlearn@aol.com*

CfBT (Centre for British Teachers), 1 The Chambers, East Street, Reading RG1 4JD. Tel: 0118-952 3900. Fax: 0118-952 3939

CILT (Centre for Information on Language Teaching and Research), 20 Bedfordbury, London WC2N 4LB. Tel: 020-7379 5110. Fax: 020-7379 5082.
Email: *library@cilt.org.uk* and see *www.cilt.org.uk*

Scottish Association for Language Learning, George Herriott School, Lauriston Place, Edinburgh EH3 9EQ. Tel: 0131-229 7263

The British Council Information Centre (EFL), 5th floor, Bridgewater House, 58 Whitworth Street, Manchester M1 6BB. Tel: 0161-957 7755. Fax: 0161-957 7762.
Email: *general.enquiries@britcoun.org*
and see *www.britcoun.org*

Bookshops/libraries
Bailey Bros and Swinfen Ltd, Warner House, Folkestone, Kent CT19 6PH. Tel: 01303-56501

European Schoolbooks Ltd, The Runnings, Cheltenham GL51 9PQ. Tel: 01242-245252. Fax: 01242-224137. Email: *direct@esb.co.uk*

Good Book Guide, 24 Seward Street, London EC1V 3PS. Tel: 020-7490 0900

Grant and Cutler, 55-57 Great Marlborough Street, London W1V 2AY. Tel: 020-7734 2012. Fax: 020-7734 9272. Email: *postmaster@grant-c.demon.co.uk*

Stanfords (maps/travel), 12-14 Long Acre, Covent Garden, London WC2E 9LP. Tel: 020-7836 1321. Fax: 020-7836 0189. Email: *SALES@Stanfords.co.uk*

W & G Foyle, 113-119 Charing Cross Road, London WC2H 0EB. Tel: 020-7437 5660

Websites

Camões Institute – language and cultural information. *www.instituto-camoes.pt*

Portugal and the Portuguese language – *www.public.iastate.edu/~pedro/pt_connect.html*

The human languages page – materials, interesting links, institutions and information in the language of your choice: *www.june29.com*

King's College, London – Department of Portuguese and Brazilian studies, various links: *www.Kcl.ac.uk/depsta/humanities/pobrst/kclhp.htm*

Língua Portuguesa – key this into search motor Altavista, and you should link to many more sites.

Reading/resources

BBC series *Discovering Portuguese*, often repeated, and worth video-taping. Six programmes of background scenes of Portugal, and language, although parts need updating now.

BBC *Talk Portuguese* series.

Satellite TV, if you have access to it, will be able to reach Portuguese TV; there is an international channel called RTPi.

On-line courses, such as that offered by the University of Glasgow (UK), called 'De tudo um pouco'.

Teach Yourself Beginners Portuguese, Hodder & Stoughton

Collins Portuguese Survival Guide

Teach Yourself Portuguese Grammar, Hodder & Stoughton

REMOVALS AND PETS
Contacts

Avalon Overseas, Drury Way, Brent Park, London NW10 0JN. Tel: 020-8451 6336. Fax: 020-8451 6419. Email: *avalon@transeuro.com*

Bishops Move, Overseas House, Stewarts Road, London SW8 4UG. Tel: 020-7498 0300. Fax: 020-7498 0749. Email: *www.bishopsmove.co.uk*

Britannia, Unit 3, Wyvern Estate, Beverley Way, New Malden, Surrey KT3 4PH. Tel: 020-8336 0220. Fax: 020-8336 0961. Email: *www.britannia_movers.co.uk*

Charles M Willie and Co (Shipping) Ltd, Celtic House, Brittania Road, Cardiff CF1 5LS. Tel: 029-20471000

Copsey Removals, 178 Crow Lane, Romford, Essex RM7 0ES. Tel: 020-8592 1003. Fax: 01708-727305

Ferry Freighting (Manchester) Ltd, Ferry House, 24-26 Brook Street, Chedderton, Oldham OL9 6NN. Tel: 0161-626 8686

Fleet Shipping International Ltd, Tel: 020-7232 0777. Fax: 020-7232 2600. Email: *sales@fleet.demon.co.uk* and see *www.fleet-shipping.co.uk*

Gauntlett International Removals Ltd, Gauntlett House, Catteshall Road, Godalming, Surrey GU7 1NH. Tel: 01483-417766

Northovers Removals and Storage, Passfield Mill Business Park, Passfield, near Liphook, Hants. GU30 7RR. Tel: 01428-751554. Fax: 01428-751564

Overs International, Unit 8, Government Road Industrial Park, Government Road, Aldershot GU11 2DA. Tel: 01252-343646. Fax: 01252-345861

Robert Darvall Ltd, 4 Acre Road, Reading, Berkshire RG1 0SX. Tel: 01734-864422

The British Association of Removers, 3 Churchill Court, 58 Station Road, North Harrow, Middlesex HA2 7SA. Tel: 020-8861 3331. Fax: 020-8861 3332. Email: *movers@bar.co.uk*

The Old House (Removals and Warehousing) Ltd, London. Tel: 020-8947 1817. Also at: 15-17 High Street, Seaford, East Sussex BN25 1PD. Tel: 01323-892934

AIM Removals and Storage, Parque Industrial do Infante, Unit 8, EN125, Torre, 8600-256 Odeáxere. Tel: 282-799 141. Fax: 282-799 146. Email: *algarve.-movers@clix.pt* (UK Tel: 01925-575 621)

TRAVEL
Contacts

British Rail Continental Section, Victoria Station, London SW1. Tel: 020-7834 2345

Brittany Ferries, Millbay Docks, Plymouth, Devon PL1 3EW. Tel: 0990-360360

P&O European Ferries, The Continental Ferry Port, Mile End, Portsmouth PO2 8QW. Tel: 0990-980980

Spratts Animal Travel service, 756 High Road, Good-mayes, Ilford, Essex IG3 8SY. Tel: 020-8597 2415

TAP Air Portugal, Gillingham House, 38/44 Gillingham Street, London SW1P 4NP. Tel: 0845-601 0932

Voyages Jules Verne, 21 Dorset Square, London NW1 6QG. Tel: 020-7616 1000. Fax: 020-7723 8629

Simply Travel (Portugal and Madeira). Tel: 020-8541 2222

Alternative Travel Group (walking holidays), 69-71 Ban-bury Road, Oxford OX2 6PE. Tel: 01865-315680. Fax: 01865-310299

Abreu Travel Agency Ltd, 109 Westbourne Grove, London W2 4UW. Tel: 020-7229 9905. Fax: 020-7229 0274. Email: *abreu.mail@btinternet.com*

Portugalia Holidays, 94 Fortis Green Road, London N2 9EY. Tel: 020-8444 1857

Faro Airport. Tel: 289-818281

Stagecoach Portugal, Lisbon. Tel: 21-483 2055

Instituto de Promoção Turística, Rua Alexandre Hercu-lano 51-2, 1200 Lisboa. Tel: 21-681174

CP – Caminhos de Ferro Portugueses (National Rail-ways), Av. da República 66, 1000 Lisboa. Tel: 21-793 1633

Via Directa (cheap travel), Arcadas de S.João, Areias de S.João. Tel: 289-580 440. Fax: 289-580 449. Email: *sales@viadirecta.net*

Websites

Portuguese tourist office: *www.portugalinsite.pt*

TAP: *www.TAP-AirPortugal.pt*

Voyages Jules Verne: *www.vjv.co.uk*

Simply Travel: *www.simplytravel.com*

Portuguese railways: *www.cp.pt*

OFFICIALDOM
Tax/work departments
Inland Revenue Claims Branch, Foreign Division, Merton Road, Bootle L69 9BL. Tel: 0151-922 6363

Inland Revenue, Inspector of Foreign Dividends, Lynwood Road, Thames Ditton, Surrey.

Department for Education and Employment (DfEE), Sanctuary Buildings, Great Smith Street, London SW1P 3BT. Tel: 020-7925 5555.
Email: *info@dfee.gov.uk*

DGCI Direcção Geral de Contribuições e Impostos (Tax Office), Rua da Alfândega 5, 1100 Lisboa. Tel: 21-887 9961

Health
BUPA International, Russell Mews, Brighton BN7 2NE. Tel: 01273-208181. Fax: 01273-866583. Algarve local adviser Tel: 282-471 169

Department of Health Leaflets Unit, PO Box 21, Honeypot Lane, Stanmore, Middlesex HA7 1AY. Tel: 0800-555777

DSS Benefits Agency, Pensions and Overseas Benefits Directorate, Incapacity Benefits Section, Tyneview Park, Whitely Road, Newcastle-upon-Tyne NE98 1BA

Exeter Friendly Society (Medical Insurance), Beech Hill, Walnut Gardens, Exeter, Devon EX4 4DG. Tel: 01392-477210

Harley Medical Services, 177A Harley Street, London W1N 1DH. Tel: 020-7935 1536

Healthsearch Ltd (medical insurance advice), 9 Newland Street, Rubgy CV22 7BJ. Tel: 01788-541855

Medical Advisory Services for Travellers Abroad Ltd

(MASTA), Bureau of PPP, Eynsham House, Tunbridge Wells, Kent TN1 2PL. Tel: 01892-512345

RNIB, Head Office, 224 Great Portland Street, London W1N 6AA. Tel; 020-7388 1266. Fax: 020-7388 2034

Royal National Institute for Deaf People, 19-23 Featherstone Street, London EC1Y 8SL. Tel: 020-7296 8000. Fax: 020-7296 8199. Minicom: 020-7296 8001

Social Security Agency, Incapacity Benefits Branch, Castle Court, Royal Avenue, Belfast BT1 1UB

Henley Wright Repatriation Services (funerals), 221 Upper Richmond Road, Putney, London SW15 6SQ. Tel: 020-8788 5303. Fax: 020-8788 2525

PPP, Eynsham House, Tunbridge Wells, Kent TN1 2PL. Tel: 01892-512345

International Relations/Social Security Benefits, Departamento de Relações Internacionais e Convenções de Segurança Social, Rua da Junqueira 112, 1302 Lisboa.

The British Hospital, Rua Saraiva de Carvalho 49, 1200 Lisboa. Tel: 21-395 5067

Clínica Médica Internacional de Cascais, Largo Luís de Camões 67-2, Cascais. Tel: 21-484 5317

Dr. Otfried Gembella, Rua Sotto Major 7-2, 8000 Faro.

Médico Dental Clinic, Hotel Rochas II, Praia da Rocha, Portimão, Algarve.

Lloyd e Whyte Insurance brokers, Maritenda House, EN125, Maritenda, Boliqueime, 8100 Loulé. Tel: 289-360 578. Fax: 289-366 472.
Email: *lloydandwhyte@ip.pt*

Luzdoc International Medical Service, Rua 25 de Abril, 12, 8600-174 Luz, Lagos. Tel: 282-780 700. Fax: 282-780 709. Email: *luzdoc@mail.telepac.pt*

The Holistic Healing Centre, Rocha Brava. Tel: 282-359
641

Multiclínica Medefi Dental Clinic, Largo Miguel Bom-
barda 3 r/c, 8400-347 Lagoa. Tel/fax: 282-341 482.
Email: *medefi@oninet.pt*

Hospital Particular (private) do Algarve, Alvor. Tel: 282-
420 400. Email: *info@hpalg.com*

Driving

AA, Fanum House, Basingstoke, Hampshire RG21 2EA

Manor Car Storage, PO Box 28, Clavering, Saffron
Walden, Essex CB11 4RA. Tel: 01799-550021

RAC, Landsdowne Road, Croydon, Surrey CR9 2JA

Almar Rent-a-car, 131 Westbourne Park Road, London
W2. Tel: 020-7243 1905. Email: *sales@almar.abcnet.-
co.uk*

Automóvel Club de Portugal (ACP), Rua Rosa Araújo 24/
6, 1250 Lisboa. Tel: 21-396 3931

United Textalgarve Lda (Importing), Rua 5 de Outubro
42, Almancil, Algarve. Tel: 289-395747. Fax: 289-
395688

Education

European Council of International Schools, 21b Lavant
Street, Petersfield, Hants. GU2 3EL. Tel: 01730-
268244. Email: *ecis@ecis.org*

Ministry of Education Secondary Department: Departamento do Ensino Secundário, Av.da Boavista, 1311-5,
4100 Porto. Tel: 02-600 26 10. Higher Education
Department: Departamento do Ensino Superior, Av.
Duque de Ávila 137-4, 1050 Lisboa. Tel: 01-354 72 70.

Employment and training network: Instituto do Emprego

e Formação Profissional (IEFP), Av. José Malhoa 11, 1070 Lisboa. Tel: 01-727 31 23

BBC Broadcasting Support Services (information on Portuguese studies in UK), 252 Western Avenue, London W3 6WJ. Tel: 020-7992 5522

National Institute for Youth, Agência Nacional Instituto Português da Juventude, Av.da Liberdade 194, 1250 Lisboa. Tel: 21-315 1961. Fax: 21-315 1959

Vocational Training for Handicrafts, CEARTE, Zona Industrial da Pedrulha, Apt. 8146, 3020 Coimbra. Tel: 239-492399

Protocol Vocational Training for Journalists, CENJOR, Rua Júlio de Andrade 5, 1150 Lisboa. Tel: 21-8853786. Fax: 21-8853355

Ministério da Educação, Gabinete de Relações Internacionais, Av. 5 de Outubro 35-37, 1000 Lisboa

Cambridge School (EFL), Praça da República 15, Coimbra

Red Tape – Gracy Biss, Rua Viveiro, Lote 4, 3D, Edif. Jardim, Apt.7, 8401-901 Lagoa. Tel: 282-341 888. Fax: 282-085 259. Email: *gracy.biss@netvisao.pt*

Websites

Education: *www.educare.pt*

Family medicine: *www.come.to/medicodefamilia*

Portuguese Embassy in London various links: *www.portembassy.gla.ac.uk*

Open University (Lisbon): *www.univ-ab.pt*

Portuguese Ministry of Education: *www.min-edu.pt*

Politics: *www.citi.pt/cultura/index*

Politicians: *www.portugal-info.net*

All the Portuguese Ministries have links under:

www.pcm.gov.pt
Law: *www.jurinfor.pt*
'Citizens shop': *www.lojadocidadao.pt*
Information on the Municipalities: *www.anmp.pt*
The President: *www.presidneciarepublica.pt*
Parliament: *www.parlamento.pt*
Government cabinet: *www.primeiro-ministro.gov.pt*
BUPA International: *www.bupa.com/int*
Portuguese Automobile Club: *www.acp.pt*
The Pensions Service (UK): *www.thepensionservice.gov.uk*
Insurance/health insurance: *www.lloydandwhyte.info*
Private hospital: *www.hospitalparticulardoalgarve.pt*

Reading/resources

Portugal Matters! Photocopiable resource on all aspects
of Portugal, from Education Matters, 29 High Street,
Halberton, Tiverton, Devon EX16 7AF, UK

Portugal: Basic Data, and Portugal: the Infrastructures
booklets produced for potential investors, available
from ICEP, the Portuguese Trade and Tourism Offices
(address given previously)

Notes and advice on driving in Portugal, and residence,
available from your nearest Portuguese consulate

Living and Working in Portugal, Sue Tyson-Ward (3rd edn
How To Books, 2002)

*Retirement: A guide to benefits for people who are retiring
or have retired/State Pensions Your Guide/Widowed? A
basic guide* (GL14), from The Pension Service,
Department for Work and Pensions

Financial help if you work or are looking for help (WK1),
from Social Security Office

LIFE IN PORTUGAL
Contacts

Portuguese UK Chamber of Commerce, 4th floor, 22/25a Sackville Street, London W1X 1DE. Tel: 020-7494 1844.

Portuguese Industrial Association: Associação Industrial Portuguesa, Praça das Indústrias, Pavilhão da FIL, 1300 Lisboa Codex. Website: *www.aip.pt*

ICEP Information on business opportunities: ICEP, Direcção de Informação, Av. 5 de Outubro, 101, 1050-051 Lisboa. Tel: 21-790 9500.
Website: *www.icep.pt*

General Sports Council: Direcção Geral de Desportos, Av. Infante Santo, 74-4, 1300 Lisboa

Portuguese Equestrian Federation: Federação Equestre Portuguesa, Av. Duque D'Ávila 9-4, 1000 Lisboa

Golf Federation: Fed. Portuguesa de Golfe, Rua Almeida Brandão 39, 1200 Lisboa.

Tennis Federation: Fed. Portuguesa de Ténis, Estádio Nacional, Caxias, 2480 Oeiras.

Fishing: Clube de Amadores de Pesca de Portugal, Rua do Salitre 175 r/c, 1200 Lisboa. Tel: 21-684805

Sailing: Fed. Portuguesa da Vela, Doca de Belém, 1300 Lisboa.

Vale de Ferro Riding Centre. Tel: 282-968 444. Fax: 282-968 443

Pinetrees Riding Centre, Almancil. Tel: 289-394 369. Email: *pinetrees.riding@clix.pt*

Marc Electrónica (TVs), Sítio do Poço Seco, Armazém 5, Cardosas, 8500-338 Portimão. Tel: 282-410 400. Fax: 282-410 406. Email: *info@tv2029.com*

Digisat (TVS), Rua do Calvário 100, 8135-123 Almancil.

Tel: 289-399 839. Fax: 289-992 063.
Email: *digisat-tv@mail.telepac.pt*

Websites

Fashion *www.citi.pt/cultura/moda*
Type in 'moda portuguesa' to search for fashion sites
Type in 'comida portuguesa' and 'vinho português' for food and wine
Many general sites on Portugal cover eating and drinking. Try: *www.portugal-info.net/*
Food: *www.gastronomias.com, www.ip.pt/gourmet*
Port wine: *www.ivp7*.pt
Wine Institute: *www.ivv.pt*
Cinema: *www.cinemaportugues.net*
Big Brother: *www.tvi.iol.pt*
Cinema/science/radio/theatre: *www.citi.pt/cultura/index*
Annual film festival in Oporto: *www.caleida.pt/fantasporto*
Many newspapers are on-line, here is a selection: *www.expresso.pt, www.oindependente.pt, www.jn.pt, www.dn.pt, www.publico.pt, www.euronoticias.pt*
Radio and TV stations are also available on-line; here are some: *www.rdp.pt, www.radiocomercial.pt, www.rtp.pt*
News site: *www.diariodigital.pt/matriz/htm*
Online magazine for women: *www.mulherportuguesa.com/*
Cinema: *www.7arte.net*
Portuguese railways: *www.cp.pt*
AA (cars): *www.acp.pt*
General highways: *www.dgv.pt*
Sports: *www.citi.pt/cultura/index/desporto*
Leisure: *http://lazer.publico.pt*
Beaches: *www.infopraias.com*

General sports info: *www.infodesporto.pt*
Football newspaper online: *www.abola.pt*
Secretary of State for Sport: *www.sedesporto.pt*
FC Porto: *www.fcporto.pt*
Satellite TV installation: *www.TV2029.com*
Riding centre: *www.valdeferro.com*

Reading/resources

The Portuguese Trade and Tourism Offices (ICEP) round the world have leaflets on wine and food

Portuguese cookery magazines have wonderful recipes and pictures to drool over: try the weekly *Segredos de Cozinha*

Algarve Country Cooking, Rainer Horbelt and Sonja Spindler (VIP publications 1996)

Portuguese Cooking, Hilaire Walden (Apple Press, 1994)

The Taste of Portugal, Edite Vieira – origins, anecdotes and recipes (Robinson, 1989)

Portugal's Wines and Winemakers, Richard Mayson (Ebury, 1992)

The Wines of Portugal, Jan Read (Faber & Faber, 1987)

The Story of Dow's Port, Richard Mason (Segrave Foulkes, 1999)

Wild Herbs and Happiness (Books 1 and 2): *Life in an Algarve Mountain Village*, Ruth Banks (available in bookshops in Algarve

Internet Rough Guide, Angus Kennedy

Algarve Life, Reg Reynolds (bookshops in Algarve or by email: *regvreynolds@yahoo.ca*)

REGIONAL TOURIST OFFICES

Associação de Turismo de Lisboa, Apartado 3326, 1301 904 Lisboa. Tel: 21-3610350. Fax: 21-3610359. Email: *atl@atl-turismolisboa.pt*   *www.atl-turismolisboa.pt*

Região de Turismo de Leiria/Fátima, Apartado 1115, 2401-801 Leiria. Tel: 244-823773. Fax: 244-833533. Email: *rtleiria-fátima@mail.telepac.pt* *www.leiriafátima-rt.pt*

Região de Turismo do Oeste, Rua Direita, 2510 Óbidos. Tel: 262-955060. Fax: 262-955061. Email: *r.t.oeste@mail.telepac.pt*   *www.cibermarket.pt*

Região de Turismo do Ribatejo, Campo Infante da Câmara, Casa do Campino, 2000-014 Santarém. Tel: 243-330330. Fax: 243-330340.

Região de Turismo de Setúbal, Travessa Frei Gaspar, 10, 2900-388 Setúbal. Tel: 265-539120. Fax: 265-539127. Email: *costa.azul@mail.telepac.pt* *www.costa-azul.rts.pt*

Região de Turismo dos Templários, Rua Serpa Pinto 1, 2300 Tomar. Tel: 249-329000. Fax: 249-324322.

Divisão de Turismo da Câmara Municipal de Sintra, Edifício do Turismo, Praça da República, 23, 2710-616 Sintra. Tel: 21-9231157. Fax: 21-9235176. Email: *cm.sintra@mail.telepac.pt www.cm-sintra.pt*

Junta de Turismo da Costa do Estoril, Arcadas do Parque, 2769-503 Estoril. Tel: 21-4664414. Fax: 21-4672280. Email: *estorilcoast@mail.telepac.pt* *www.estorilcoast-tourism.com*

Comissão Municipal de Turismo do Porto, Rua Clube dos Fenianos, 25, 4000 Porto. Tel: 22-3393470. Fax: 22-3323303.

Região de Turismo do Alto Minho, Castelo de Santiago

da Barra, 4900-360 Viana do Castelo. Tel: 258-820270.Fax: 258-829798.
Email: *rtam@mail.telepac.pt www.rtam.pt*
Região de Turismo do Alto Tâmega e Barroso, Avenida Tenente Valadim, 39-1 Dto., 5400 Chaves. Tel: 276-340660. Fax: 276-321419.
Email: *rturismoatb@mail.telepac.pt*
Região de Turismo do Douro Sul, Rua dos Bancos Apartado 36, 5101 Lamego Codex. Tel: 254-615770. Fax: 254-614014.
Email: *douro turismo@mail.telepac.pt*
Região de Turismo do Nordeste Transmontano, Largo do Principal, 5300-054 Bragança. Tel: 273-331078. Fax: 273-331913. *www.bragancanet.pt/turismo*
Região de Turismo da Serra do Marão, Av. 1 de Maio, 70-1C, 5000-651 Vila Real. Tel: 259-322819. Fax: 259-321712. Email: *turismomarao@mail.telepac.pt*
Região de Turismo do Verde Minho, Praça Dr.José ferreira Salgado, 90-6, 4704-525 Braga. Tel: 252-202770. Fax: 253-202779.
Email: *rtvm@mail.telepac.pt www.rtvm.pt*
Região de Turismo do Centro, Largo da Portagem, 3000-337 Coimbra. Tel: 239-855930. Fax: 239-25576.
Região de Turismo de Dão Lafões, Av. Gulbenkian, 3510-055 Viseu. Tel: 232-420950. Fax: 232-8420957.
Email: *rt-dao-lafoes@mail.telepac.pt*
www.autonet.pt/rt-dao-lafoes
Região de Turismo da Rota da Luz, Rua João Mendonça, 8, 3800-200 Aveiro. Tel: 234-423680. Fax: 234-428326.
Região de Turismo da Serra da Estrela, Av. Frei Heitor Pinto, 6200 Covilhã. Tel: 275-319560. Fax: 275-319569. Email: *telepac.pt-www.rt-serradaestrela.pt*

www.turismo-estrela
Região de Turismo de Évora, Rua de Aviz, 90, 7000-591
Évora. Tel: 266-742534. Fax: 266-705238.
Região de Turismo da Planície Dourada, Praça da
República, 12, 7800-427 Beja. Tel: 284-310150. Fax:
284-310151. Email: *rtpd@mail.telepac.pt*
www.eurowrite.edu/rtpd
Região de Turismo de São Mamede, Estrada de Santana,
25, 7300 Portalegre. Tel: 245-300770. Fax: 245-20453.
Email: *rt.s.mamede@mail.telepac.pt www.rstm.pt*
Região de Turismo do Algarve, Av. 5 de Outubro, 18,
Apartado 106, 8001-902 Faro. Tel: 289-800400. Fax:
289-800489. Email: *rtalgarve@rtalgarve.pt*
www.rtalgarve.pt
Direcção Regional do Turismo, Rua Comendador
Ernesto Rebelo, 14, 9900-501 Horta (Faial). Tel:
292-200500. Fax: 292-200501.
Email: *acoresturismo@mail.telepac.pt*
www.drtacores.pt
Direcção Regional do Turismo, Avenida Arriaga, 18,
9004-519 Funchal. Tel: 291-229057. Fax: 291-232151.
Email: *drtpromarekting@mail.telepac.pt*
www.madinfo.pt/drturismo

BRITISH CONSULATES OFFICES IN PORTUGAL

British Embassy, Consular section, Rua de São Bernardo,
33, 1249-082 Lisboa. Tel: 21-392 4160. Fax: 21-392
4188.
Email: *consular@fco.gov.uk www.uk-embassy-pt*
British Consulate, Avenida da Boavista, 3072, 4100-120
Porto. Tel: 22-618 4789. Fax: 22-610 0438.
Email: *oporto@fco.gov.uk*

Brit. Consulate, Largo Francisco A Maurício, 7-1, 8500-535 Portimão. Tel: 282-417800. Fax: 282-417806. Email: *britcon.portimão@mail.telepac.pt*

Brit. Consulate, EC Zarco (Funchal), PO Box 417, 9001-905 Funchal, Madeira. Tel: 291-221221. Fax: 291-233789. Email: *Brit.Confunchal@mail.eunet.pt*

Brit. Consulate, Quinta do Bom Jesus, 23, Rua das Almas, Pico da Pedra, 9600-069 Ribeira Grande, São Miguel, Açores. Tel: 296-498115. Fax: 296-498330.

Index